Foreword b
Major Ge
Preside..., ..., ...

THE
BRONZE
SCAR

Understanding How PTSD Feels
to Help Victims and Those Who
Support Them

DR. STEVE WEST

Chaplain, Colonel, USAF (Ret)

THE BRONZE SCAR
Understanding How PTSD Feels to Help Victims and Those Who Support Them
© 2021 Dr. Steve West

Published by C&S Publishing | Pelham, Alabama
ISBN (Paperback): 979-8-9891246-0-2
ISBN (Hardback): 979-8-9891246-1-9
ISBN (EPub): 979-8-9891246-2-6
Printed in the United States of America
Prepared for Publication: www.wendykwalters.com

DISCLAIMER

The information provided in this book is designed to provide helpful information on the subjects discussed. This book is not meant to be used, nor should it be used, to diagnose or treat any medical condition. For diagnosis or treatment of any medical problem, consult your own physician.

TO CONTACT THE AUTHOR: **www.bronzescar.com**

Dedication

For all of those who suffer from PTSD
who continuously carry a heavy weight,
and for our families, as they carry
the person carrying that weight.

Success is not final, failure is not fatal:
it is the courage to continue that counts.

Winston Churchill

Praise for The Bronze Scar

"Walk into the head of PTSD. See the thoughts. Feel the emotions. Experience the reality. Steve West opens the hidden hallways for all to explore. This book gives a rare journey into the secrets of how yesterday's traumas shape all of today's life into tomorrow.

The Bronze Scar answers questions we didn't know how to ask. Candid. Raw. Compassionate. These pages are for the circles of PTSD from personal to family, friends, and professionals."

—Leith Anderson
President Emeritus, National Association of Evangelicals, Washington, DC

"Rarely does one find a 'man's man' such as Colonel Steve West willing to be vulnerable enough to share a personal struggle that could negatively impact other people's perception of him. In *The Bronze Scar*, he is real, raw, and ready to make a difference in the lives of fellow sufferers as he navigates his path out of PTSD. Timely and gripping, this book resonated with me, having been plagued with unrelenting memories of a home invasion that occurred years ago. Steve has the solution for breaking free. Read this book and share it!"

—Deborah Smith Pegues
International Speaker,
Bestselling Author of Emergency Prayers and Forgive, Let Go, and Live

"I have no doubt that PTSD is one of the reasons we aren't making more headway in the war against homelessness. Unless we all become fully cognizant of this condition and know how to recognize it in those around us, the anxiety, anger, and shame that Steve West describes will continue to drive far too many of our friends onto the streets and into addictions that will only make things worse. I'm strongly recommending that *The Bronze Scar* be on the required reading list for all of the leaders of North America's rescue missions and kindred ministries."

—John Ashmen

President, Citygate Network

"During great pain and suffering, we usually ask ourselves two questions: 'Is there help?' and, 'Is there hope?' In his book, *The Bronze Scar*, Steve West declares a resounding 'Yes!' Through personal storytelling and pastoral shepherding, Steve West gives the reader help and hope. I commend this compelling book for giving you wisdom, insight, and encouragement to persevere—no matter what challenges you face."

—Dr. Kenneth Bruce

Senior Pastor, Westwood Baptist Church, Alabaster, Alabama

"Steve writes with vulnerability and honesty about the trials of living with PTSD. *The Bronze Scar* is a powerful resource that will help those living with PTSD as well as the families who walk this journey alongside them."

—Meredith Dunn

Founder and CEO, Freedom Press

'My Dad lived with PTSD for 60 years before finally acknowledging the trauma he endured from the Korean War. Steve lays bare for all to see the realities of what our brave service members, including my dad, endure during wartime. It takes a lot of courage to admit the negative psychological impacts of war, especially for a chaplain whose very mission is to help others. *The Bronze Scar* is a book about courage, discovery, family, and faith. It is a vivid depiction of what thousands of war survivors deal with every day. A must-read for those in and out of the military."

—General (Ret) Larry O. Spencer
37th Vice Chief of Staff of the Air Force, Author of Dark Horse, General Larry O. Spencer and His Journey from the Horseshoe to the Pentagon.

"I want to thank Dr. West for baring his soul through this PTSD journey. His intimate knowledge of the PTSD experience has enhanced my understanding and sensitivity to those burdened by this disability. *The Bronze Scar* is a must-read for anyone who seeks to counsel or assist those with PTSD."

—William B. Dowling
Licensed Professional Counselor (LPC)

"I got to know Steve and Cherri when he was in the depth of his PTSD struggle. I personally saw the grip it had on his life and the impact on his job and his family. *The Bronze Scar* is a testimony of God's grace and strength in his life and his wife's determination to hold true to her wedding vow to 'love and cherish ... in sickness and health.' Their story will be a beacon of hope to many."

—Jim Browning
Director of the Marsh Center for Chaplain Studies; Ch, Col (Ret) USAF

"I have known Steve West since Christmas Eve of 1974 when we were both young Airmen stationed in Las Vegas. I am eternally grateful to him for sharing the gospel with me on that very day. My life took a 180° turn for the better because of his witness. Now I'm 47 years older and a mental health professional. I have treated many with PTSD who seem to have given up hope of getting better. I feel *The Bronze Scar* will help many. I endorse it wholeheartedly."

—Mark C. Harol

MS, LMHCS, USAF Retired

"Steve cares deeply about helping others. I've personally experienced the power of his empathetic approach to fostering personal and professional growth. In *The Bronze Scar,* he articulates the struggles those suffering from PTSD experience with the clarity and focus that only someone who's been through it can offer. Steve's self-awareness and honesty around the internal dissonance arising from his faith and PTSD allow for a truly transformational work that gives the reader permission to recognize the tensions that may exist in their own lives."

—Augusta Love Rutledge

Host of the Acclaimed Podcast FedUpward

"*The Bronze Scar* reveals the often-invisible cost paid by so many people who suffer PTSD. Steve West knows the impact of paying this price firsthand, but more importantly, he understands how personal faith in God facilitates healing. This book is an incredible resource for people wrestling with PTSD as well as those who love and support them. Highly recommended!"

—Chris Hodges
Senior Pastor, Church of the Highlands,
Author of The Daniel Dilemma and Out of the Cave

"*The Bronze Scar* is an extraordinary testimonial of courage and selfless disclosure, shining a light on a very dark and personal struggle impacting today's warriors and so many more in our society. Readers who are suffering from PTSD will see themselves in Steve's experience and, through their newfound awareness, finally have a road map to address the pain underlying their behavior before it destroys their family, their career, and ultimately their life."

—Bonnie Carroll
President & Founder, Tragedy Assistance Program For Survivors (TAPS)

"Steve and I have been close friends since 1996. His willingness to write *The Bronze Scar* is a glorious example of God causing all things to work together for good to those who love Him and are called according to His purpose (Romans 8:28). I think millions who deal with PTSD will benefit from Steve's book; therefore, I am using it as a textbook to educate and train chaplains."

—Dr. Ronald M. Harvell Brigadier General, USAF (Ret)
Foundational Director of the Dewey Center for Chaplaincy and Professor at
Charleston Southern University

"In our family there were the knowing looks, holding your breath, avoiding certain topics of conversation, and the desire to help complicated by the fear of what your concerns might provoke. Our Marine arrived home from Afghanistan with 2 Purple Hearts and a deep soul wound. He grimaced with physical pain, but the torment of the PTSD was equally as bad. I had no idea what he was feeling. There is so much in this book I wish I had known a decade ago. I would have been better able to understand what my Marine was feeling. If you have longed for someone to open a window into the complex world of feelings associated with PTSD, *The Bronze Scar* is for you."

—Carmen LaBerge

Radio Host for Faith Radio, Author

"Chaplain Steve West's work on PTSD is a wonderful story of hope and healing. Being vulnerable, he shares his struggle with PTSD. Yet, Dr. West does not leave us hanging. He combines insights from science and other fields to give practical advice on how PTSD can be treated. *The Bronze Scar* is a great resource for individuals, families, and care providers to give hope and healing to those in the middle of the struggle."

—The Rt. Rev. Page Brooks, Ph.D.

Lead Pastor-Missio Mosaic: A Missional Society/Network, Professor of Theology and Culture, State Command Chaplain (LTC), Louisiana Army National Guard

Contents

# ACKNOWLEDGMENTS

At first glance it may seem like I alone am the author of this book. Yes, this is *my* journey with PTSD. Yet without some very special people, this undertaking would not have been possible to bring to completion. I have not done this alone. Many have encouraged me to write, while others have given me direction. Some have been driving forces, pushing me to put words and feelings to paper.

There are a few with whom I would like to pull back the curtain and express my gratitude. My wife, Cherri, has walked through this journey with me. She has had to endure moods, anger, verbal abuse, and abandonment. Without her and my daughter Jenni I might have never sought help. Thank you for being key figures in my initial acknowledgment that I have PTSD in my life. My son Adam continues to provide me much needed encouragement along the way. I'm so thankful for this family!

I also want to recognize that there are people who have played significant roles in my finally accomplishing this project. My co-workers with the National Association of Evangelicals for encouraging me to write. Also, good friends who contributed, many times, without realizing they had done anything.

I could never have completed this book without an empowering team of professionals. Meredith Dunn, my author coach, who challenged me throughout the process of making me a better writer. Stephanie Spector as copy editor, for helping so much by making the manuscript read like a book. Wendy Walters, who took the manuscript and handled all production tasks until the book was a reality.

Most of all, I thank God that He has walked close beside me, held my hand, and carried me at times, filling me with the inspiration to write. None of this is possible without Him.

FOREWORD

D o n d i   E .   C o s t i n ,   P h . D .

Major General, U.S. Air Force (Ret)
President, Liberty University

Napoleon Bonaparte once observed that a soldier will fight long and hard to earn a bit of colored ribbon to place on his uniform. On another occasion he is alleged to have said that he could conquer the world if he had enough ribbons to place on the tunics of his soldiers.

Having invested more than 36 years of my own life in uniform, I can attest that Napoleon was right. He was right because warriors love to win and will do whatever it takes to defeat the enemy. Willing to risk life and limb for their comrades and their cause, they soldier on until the job is done and the battle is won. Such is the nature of war.

While warfighters don't fight for the ribbon, the thought of adding another ribbon to the rack certainly doesn't hurt, especially in a line of work that requires its practitioners to wear their resumes as ribbon racks on their chests. Even so, the ribbon is never the end itself but is often a helpful means to that end. Such is the nature of the warrior.

The challenge for many warriors—and their chaplains—is that the war does not end when that bit of colored cloth finds its home on the rack. Understandably, that fact never graces the glossy brochures and social media campaigns recruiters use to fill the ranks. For some reason, it doesn't lodge in the heads of heroes during training. Even when it does, many of their fears are dulled the minute they lock arms with their battle buddies, put their minds on the mission, and place their finger on the trigger. It's just what warriors do; it's why we call them heroes.

Once the fighting is finished, a lucky few never think of the horrors of war again. Miraculously, they just move on. Most of us find our minds muddied once in a while, yet somehow, we never dwell on the worst parts for long. But some trauma survivors can think of nothing else.

For reasons that can seldom be explained to our satisfaction, the heroics of some warriors leave lasting wounds, even among the most patriotic, the bravest, the strongest, and the best prepared. In this imperfect world, trauma takes a toll. The inner life of these survivors on the other side of their trauma barely resembles life before the fall. Their inability to get better is frustrating, uncomfortable, and inexplicable for themselves and their families. Which means they often suffer in silence until someone raises their hand to say that it's OK not to feel OK.

The heroics of some warriors leave lasting wounds, even among the most patriotic, the bravest, the strongest, and the best prepared.

I can think of no better example of this reality than Chaplain, Colonel Steve West, who has raised his hand by writing this monumental book. In God's providence, I was Steve's supervisor as a lieutenant colonel when then-Major West went to war. I helped keep an eye on his family while he was deployed, and I was there when he came home. Something changed in the months between his tearful goodbye and his joyful reunion, but nobody could put their finger on what that something was. Especially Steve. None of us knew then that hidden beneath his hard-earned and well-deserved Bronze Star medal was a hard-to-describe yet life-altering bronze scar. A capable chaplain left home to do his duty. A wounded warrior returned.

A skilled staff officer, decorated military leader, and expert therapist who had made a career of helping others, he came home with battle scars so deep that, for the first time in his life, he could not help himself. As a result, he found that he was not as effective when it came to helping others. Of all the intolerable elements of his post-traumatic stress, the latter was the most intolerable for him.

Having counseled many trauma survivors through the years, the sense of being unable to help oneself and others makes life harder than it should be. The complex of menacing maladies that still haunt Steve come forth in this book with a power that is impossible to describe unless you have lived in his head for a while. Reading this book will be revealing for all and healing for many.

Steve lays bare in these pages what being traumatized feels like. He wrestles openly with extreme pain that leads to extraordinary insight. Which is why this book is not so much about war or war stories as it is the war within.

Because I know the author and the path he has traveled, I can say with conviction that it is most importantly a book about how to win that war. And because I have heard the stories of those who have experienced every form of imaginable trauma, I can confidently say that this book will be a treasure to anyone living with the pain of trauma, regardless of its source. You may not immediately find the answer to every question, but you will find the courage to ask the right ones. You will find the words to name your vexing issues and the way to claim them as your own.

When Albert Einstein was asked how he would apportion his time if he had but one hour to solve a wicked problem, he reportedly said that he would spend 55 minutes defining the problem and the last five minutes solving it. *The Bronze Scar* lets us look over Steve's shoulder during the 55 minutes of his golden hour. His courage in giving us this front-row seat is a gift to anyone ever traumatized by any means, to friends and family who have not yet found a way to understand the pain of their loved one, and to caregivers looking for just the right words to make sense of the senseless.

Now that Steve has poured out his soul for his sake and ours, he can remove any doubt in his mind as to how helpful he has been to others on this side of his darkest days. For in his struggle, you can make sense of your own. You can be certain that you are not the only one who feels the way you do. Finally, you can know that you are not alone.

DONDI E. COSTIN, Ph.D.
Major General, U.S. Air Force, (Ret)
President, Liberty University

PREFACE

A m I crazy? That's one of the questions I ask myself from time to time. Not being able to control my actions, memories, anxiety, and other aspects as a result of PTSD is what causes me to ponder this question. I know the answer is no. I just can't reconcile who I am now and what I've become compared to who I was and how I acted before all of this.

I'm writing this book so that people who have PTSD who read this will realize they're not alone. I've tried to be transparent and speak from my heart. I've written what goes through my head and how I feel at any given moment, hoping it will resonate. My wish is for readers to recognize these thoughts and feelings in themselves and gain insight, making the thoughts and feelings easier to explain to other people.

Writing for those who have PTSD is not my only goal. I'd also like this to help families, friends, and co-workers who deal with the imbalances on a daily basis. By detailing my experiences, I hope that people can gain a better understanding of what's really happening when someone with PTSD's anxiety rises. How are they really feeling? One of the great disadvantages of living with someone with PTSD is having no point of reference. Not being able to relate to a loved one with PTSD brings on its own frustrations. In the world of PTSD, the ones who invest themselves in us are oftentimes the ones we lash out at and hurt the most. So if this book helps explain how PTSD feels, then sufferers and their families can hopefully understand each other a little better. Even if this book just brings us to the point where we can intelligently talk about this experience, that's a positive enough starting point for me.

Yet another group I'm writing to is the group of people who are not sure if they have PTSD, and so haven't reached out for help. If they're able to identify with what I share, then my prayer is that it will lead them to seek help. This cannot be done alone. It takes a group of people committed to the one person who suffers from PTSD. Not everyone can be cured, but everyone can find some level of healing. That healing comes from understanding the inner turmoil and outward manifestations of PTSD.

This book has been a long time in the making. It took me over two years to write. Add to that the ten years where I kept so much of my story bottled up. It has been a hard journey—pouring myself out, being honest about my faults and negativity. But if it helps people, the struggle is worth it.

A man was walking down a deserted beach early one morning. In the distance, he spotted another man throwing something into the ocean. Over and over, the man would reach down, pick up something, and toss it into the water. The walker came up to the man and asked what he was doing.

"See these starfish washed up on the shore?" said the man who was throwing. "The tide has gone out, and they have no way to get back to the water. If they are not in the water by the time the sun gets hot, they will dry out and die. I'm just helping them back into the water."

Looking around the beach, the man who had happened upon this scene could see many starfish trapped on the shore. "That's crazy," he said. "There are thousands of starfish left on the sand. What makes you think it will make any difference?"

Without saying a word, the man reached down, picked up another starfish, and threw it into the water. "It made a difference to that one!"

My ultimate goal for this book is to explain how I feel; if that makes a difference to those affected by PTSD, I will be happy.

PTSD: It's not the person refusing to let go of the past, but the past refusing to let go of the person.

HealthyPlace.com

BRONZE STAR CITATION

Chaplain, Lieutenant Colonel Steven E. West distinguished himself in trauma ministry in Iraq, conducting 1,707 critical visit hours for 2,766 emergencies, including 1,665 combat casualties. Chaplain West personally ministered to numerous victims of a mass casualty suicide bombing, including a young child who died in his arms. From September 10, 2007 to March 18, 2008, he provided comfort to Balad Air Base Airmen in the face of great adversity. He administered 1,930 counseling sessions by meritorious achievement as the Wing Chaplain, 332d Air Expeditionary Wing while supporting ground and air operations against the enemy at Balad Air Base in Iraq. During this period, while exposed to more than 200 enemy rocket and mortar attacks, Chaplain West demonstrated impeccable faith and character, providing spiritual guidance to more than 17,200 Airmen, spanning two Air Expeditionary Force rotations at four Air Bases. Under his stewardship, the chapel team orchestrated the largest number of counseling sessions: 278 combat stress cases, 21 suicide interventions, 10 next-of-kin notifications, and a dignified, compassionate memorial service for three fallen American heroes. Chaplain West directed construction of the Gilbert Memorial Chapel, a $775,000 project that supported 20 services attended by 13,500 worshipers weekly. He arranged 92 study groups and quadrupled the size of the Airmen's Center. Of particular note, Chaplain West developed and led a revolutionary chapel ministry aimed at Airmen serving at remote sites, directly supporting 1,502 Airmen assigned to duty at 61 forward operating bases. The exemplary leadership, personal endeavor, and devotion to duty displayed by Chaplain West in this responsible position reflect great credit upon himself and the United States Air Force.

As it turns out, the greatest honor in my life was when I was awarded with the Bronze Star. It also left a substantial scar that affects me to this day. Thus the title, *THE BRONZE SCAR—Understanding How PTSD Feels to Help Victims and Those Who Support Them.*

 # INTRODUCTION

Post-traumatic stress disorder, or PTSD, is not about conquering. It's about enduring.

Some people have the idea that anything short of a cure for PTSD is unacceptable, thus setting themselves up for failure. But if we accept conquering PTSD as an end goal, we can't heal. Enduring is about having the ability to refocus when something prompts negative thoughts or actions. It's realizing that none of us is perfect—we have to accept the fact that we will have flaws, we will have setbacks, and we will have failures. Incremental steps forward, no matter how small, is still progress.

When I think about my story as a military chaplain and my PTSD journey, it begins with these considerations.

I was in Iraq during the surge, when the U.S. deployed 30,000 additional troops and equipment. President Bush's strategy was, in his words, to reduce the violence enough so that "… daily life will improve, Iraqis will gain confidence in their leaders, and the government will have the breathing space it needs to make progress in other critical areas." It was a mission push throughout the country. That also meant a significant increase in the number of troops who were wounded, many catastrophically, or worse—dead.

I was the Wing Chaplain, the senior chaplain on base for the 332nd Expeditionary Wing, which the Air Force had reactivated from World War II for Iraq. When it was deactivated, it would come to be known as the Tuskegee Airmen, the "Red Tails." Because of that rich history, our motto was "The Legend Continues," and our personnel were proud of it. We weren't the original Tuskegee Airmen, but we were part of the Tuskegee Airmen Wing, and that's significant.

The trauma was like nothing I'd ever seen or experienced. And it happened every single day. Before this, I'd spent years as an Emergency Medical Technician (EMT). If you'd asked me then, I would have told you that I'd seen it all. Someone dying in front of me? I'd seen it. Pulling bodies from wrecked cars? I'd done it. Shootings? Stabbings? I have experienced all manner of situations so grotesque they turned my stomach. I've been a minister for more than forty years. I'd worked with people suffering from all kinds of trauma. During my military career, I served as a hospital chaplain twice. I was sure that because I'd had so much experience in emergency rooms and hospitals, I'd be all right. With all that experience, I thought going to a war zone would be a piece of cake. "Been there, done that," would have been my answer.

That's what I would have told you…if you'd asked me before this.

But I would have been lying to you. Because nothing compared to this nightmare. I could not have been more wrong. I could not have been more unprepared for what I would witness. With all my training and experience, still absolutely nothing could have prepared me for the ugly reality and trauma of war.

But I quickly discovered battlefield trauma affects you in an entirely different way, and that realization ate at me for a long time. Why was being in that trauma center, in that staging area, in those emergency rooms so disturbing to me? Why was I so shaken every day?

Then one day the answer came to me. Every patient who came in, every person we treated in the hospital, whether military, civilian adults, or children, had been injured by a terrorist.

Everyone I treated, everyone who suffered, and everyone who died had that common denominator—someone intentionally meant to hurt or to kill them. I knew terrorists didn't care whether they were attacking Iraqi civilians or American troops. They didn't hesitate to kill anyone who disagreed with their ideology.

I'll never forget the first time I took a patient off of a Blackhawk. We were the only air evacuation hospital in Iraq, and that's how most casualties came to us. The injured had to be transferred from the helicopter to one of those old canvas litters from past wars. Every day several Blackhawks came in simultaneously. If one came in, we knew that more were coming. You had no idea who you were picking up. I'd be sent out there with a partner. They'd tell us which helicopter approach to expect, and the aircrew would let us know which litter was ours. We'd pull it out and attach it to a gurney. We couldn't pay much attention to it. This was life and death, so we had to move fast. We took the litter fifty yards back to the emergency room and started filling the bays.

I remember that the first patient was a young Iraqi man, a civilian. At that time, I didn't know if he was a terrorist or not, but we took him in, and then two more came in while we were setting him up in the bays on each side—a U.S. Army soldier and a handcuffed insurgent. I later learned that while the young Iraqi man was talking to our soldier, the insurgent walked up and shot him. The soldier then shot the insurgent, and while he was going down, he shot the soldier. Three people shot, and they all came in together.

If people want to know what Americans are like, what this country stands for, I saw it right there in front of my eyes. The guy that we brought in first was shot first. The doctors worked just as hard on the insurgent as they did on our soldier and the Iraqi man. It didn't matter who he was, where he came from, or what his political opinions were, what faith he had, or didn't have. At that moment, I was so proud of my country and our military. I don't know what clicked that day, but I just thought there are no rules. We don't fight people who believe in the Geneva Convention. We fight insurgents who don't care about what's right or wrong.

As I went through the hospital, I saw children, mothers, and fathers who had been caught in an explosion. They were just innocent civilians, and I kept thinking about how horrible this had to be for them, and that this was what their lives were like now. They were living in a city destroyed by war. Many locations only had electricity a couple of hours per day. They were often without running water or water that was safe to drink—living conditions we've never had to endure in the United States. Thank God.

As the Wing Chaplain, I was issued a handheld radio, often referred to as a "brick," so I could be reached in the event that I was needed. I carried the radio with me everywhere, the way I carry my cell phone now. It was either in my pocket or my hand. I didn't want to miss anything. I was at the chapel, away from the hospital area, when the call went out for mass casualties. I jumped into my Air Force pick-up and drove two minutes to the hospital. I ran down the halls to the emergency room. Casualties were coming in, and I immediately realized the room was full. I had never seen nearly that number of casualties at one time. The wounded were being treated wherever there was enough space to fit a gurney. Almost fifty casualties were crammed into a room designed for fifteen patients.

You look at one patient, and it's hard. You look at another one, and it's hard. In mass casualty situations, chaplains are less focused on talking to people than they are in taking action and demonstrating Christ's compassion. We try to be visible reminders of the Holy, and to help the overwhelmed hospital staff.

I told myself that this was what controlled chaos looks like. At first it appeared to be absolute chaos, but as I continued watching, I could see that the medical personnel had a system. They all knew their jobs and how to interact with one another when working with multiple patients. They were running right and left and here and there, but I began to feel a calmness come over me. I went to one of the patients being treated. I don't even remember if he was one of our soldiers or a civilian. There was no IV pole, so I grabbed the bag as they were transferring him onto the bed and stood there holding it. At that moment, it was all I could do.

Meanwhile, the medical team was rushing all around, quickly cutting away clothing so they could get a better look at the wounds. Technicians were going from patient to patient, taking X-rays with a portable machine, working to stop bleeding, stabilize broken extremities, and calm patients. Someone had found an available IV pole and came up behind me. We hung the bag I was holding, and I tried to see where I was needed next. Beds were lined up on both sides of the bay with an aisle down the middle where medical personnel scurried from patient to patient.

From the aisle, I could see more of what was happening throughout the room. I felt great pride in my chapel team and our ministry. Everywhere I looked, I saw a chaplain or a chaplain assistant pitching in. One was putting pressure on a wound. Another held a patient's hand, trying to keep him calm, although he was in enormous pain. One was with a child, rubbing its head, and yet another was kneeling on the floor wiping up blood, so that no one would slip amid all the chaos. No one had told them what to do. They just came in and did what was needed.

I began working with an injured boy. I had never seen so many children hurting, and I found myself gravitating toward them as they came in. At some point, while I was working with a patient, a nurse came and brought me to another child. No one was around, and as we walked up, I could see a terrified boy. The nurse said, "Just talk to him. Hold his hand. Rub his forehead. Do whatever you feel is best." I don't remember what I did, but I do know that I tried to communicate with him through my expressions and compassion.

There was so much pain and suffering. The sounds seemed to intensify in my head, sounds of people working to preserve life. Orders were barked out. Personnel were shouting to be heard above the noise. The clanging as objects hit the floor and the incessant beep of medical equipment. But the most chilling sounds were the cries of dozens of people in pain. Every sound imaginable, from a moan to a whimper to weeping to screaming at the top of their lungs.

The staff bumped into each other as they moved from one patient to another. Everyone was doing something. No time to stop and catch your breath. When you finished one task, another was waiting. I have blocked or forgotten many of my actions that day.

This is what it's like to be immersed in a massive trauma. It reminds me of the movie *For the Love of the Game*, which is about an aging baseball pitcher. When he got on the mound, the crowd would yell at him. From the dugout, the other team made noises to distract him. It was too much to process, until he told himself, "Clear the mechanism." I experienced this that day, and many times afterward. The noise began fading away. I believe it's an act of God. He cleared the mechanism, and all that mattered—all I heard or saw—was the person I was trying to help.

After a little while, one of the Iraqi interpreters asked me to come with her. Someone jumped in and took over what I'd been doing. What hurts is that you forget about the person you were helping, because you suddenly have to turn your focus to someone else.

I remember hearing her tell me that a child was dying or already dead. In a trauma situation, patients who are beyond saving are called "expectant." All the medical staff can do is make them as comfortable as possible, because they have to focus on those who still have a chance to live. So, I followed the interpreter and looked down at a four or five-year-old Iraqi girl lying on a pallet on the floor.

I could tell that the precious, innocent little girl was dead. The interpreter asked me to pray. I got down on my knees and held her in my arms, hoping the staff would be comforted to see that someone was paying attention to this child. Before I knew it, someone came and asked me to help with something else. In those situations, a chaplain is needed, and someone on the staff may be going through a crisis themselves. Someone may be yelling, "I don't want to die! I don't want to die!"

The real kicker to this story is the effect it had on me. I think of that day as the Yin and Yang. I looked at my staff and thought, "This is a wonderful group of loving people willing to do whatever is needed with so much pain and trauma around them."

A couple of weeks later, the Air Force Central Command Chaplain responsible for all of the Middle East came to our base for a few days. We had a pleasant visit, showing him our ministry in action, explaining the chapel team's mission and vision.

A distinguished visitor will usually meet with the commander, so we set up an office call with our General. When the command chaplain and I arrived at headquarters, I planned to sit in the outer office, which was standard protocol, allowing the two men to speak freely, especially since the discussion related to my leadership or the chapel staff. I was thankful that the General and I had a great relationship.

When the time came for the command chaplain to go into the office, the General asked me to sit in. He said, "There's nothing I need to say that I would not want you to hear. If the command chaplain wants to discuss something in private, you can step out."

I quietly sat through the PowerPoint briefing, which outlined the mission of the base. Balad was the largest Air Base in Iraq, with the busiest trauma center. The command chaplain asked, kind of in jest, "How's this guy working out for you?"

I don't recall exactly what the General said, but it was something like, "He's one of a kind. He understands what it means to take care of people, and he has his staff doing exactly that." Then he turned to me and teased, "You can pay me later, Steve."

The command chaplain said something along the lines of "That's good to hear, because this is a hectic place, with numerous responsibilities."

What the General said in response startled me. "Yeah. But I worry about Steve some." I was thinking to myself, *I'm not going through a tough time. This is a great ministry. I'm feeling pretty good.* Then he looked at me and said, "Steve, you know you haven't been completely yourself. You've been in a lot of pain." I honestly didn't know what he meant. I thought he must be joking.

The command chaplain asked if he could help, and the General responded, "We had a mass casualty a few weeks back. Almost forty died. An Al Qaeda insurgent drove his car into the city of Balad's marketplace outside the base and detonated himself. It was a calculated attack, designed to maximize human suffering, carried out at the busiest time of day when a large crowd was buying and selling.

Then he said something that hit me. "A four-year-old Iraqi girl died in Steve's arms."

"A four-old Iraqi girl died in Steve's arms."

I interrupted the General. "No. I prayed for a four-year-old Iraqi girl who had died from the blast just minutes before I got there."

"Chaplain West," the General said, "That's not true. Hospital staff told me that an interpreter took you to the room where this expectant child was lying. She was in a great deal of pain, and she was terrified. The medical staff had done all they could do to comfort her. You didn't say a word. You immediately dropped to your knees and scooped her up in your arms. Then you told the interpreter that the girl was scared, and you wouldn't let her die without someone holding her."

"No, sir," I insisted, "That's not what happened. She was already dead when I got there."

He looked straight at me and said, "You're wrong. They said you were there about ten minutes before she died, and you comforted her and held her close until the end."

I was shocked. Eleven years later, all I remember is that she was dead, and I prayed. No matter what I do or how hard I try, I can't remember anything else.

I didn't want credit for something I hadn't done, so I went to a nurse who had been in the trauma center that day. She said, "I was doing something else at the time, but that's what people who were with you have told me."

I've begged the Lord to give me back the whole memory, but He has not seen fit to do so. The memory of her lifeless body in my arms is not what I want. I want more. I have prayed to God and even yelled at Him. "Why would you do this? Just let me see her alive. Let me remember something to trigger it. Let me remember her living. Lord, please give me that." Still, nothing changes. God has been silent. I live with an emotional hole in my chest, and I guess it's never going to heal.

I have no idea why God hasn't granted my request. The Bible tells us

He wants us to have the desires of our hearts, but that doesn't mean He always gives us those desires and never turns a deaf ear to our requests. Sometimes He says "no," or "not yet."

In my early twenties, when, as an Airman, I was stationed at Nellis Air Force Base, Las Vegas, Nevada, I was in my car listening to a Christian radio station that was running a call-in pledge drive. A woman called in and gave her testimony of how God provided money for her to give each year.

She began by saying, "I have a jar in my kitchen window, and every time God answers a prayer, I put a quarter in the jar."

I wanted to reach into the radio and yell, "That's not how God works! He answers every prayer! You're saying that you put in a quarter every time God says 'yes.' Some of the time, He says 'no.' What you ought to do is put a quarter in the jar every time you pray."

My memory may not return to me on this side of heaven. I have accepted that, for whatever reason, He is saying, "Trust Me, Steve, I'm doing this for you."

Some memories grab me, because I went through so much in those times, all so gut-wrenching. I remember the twenty-year-old Marine from St. Louis, Missouri, whose medical team called me in. They had assembled an Angel Team—the doctors, nurses, and technicians who had been trying to save a life. When the patient is beyond saving and only the ventilator is keeping them alive, before they turn it off, the team will call the chaplain to read scripture and say a prayer.

In the case of the young Marine, although the injuries were caused by a blast, they were internal, not outwardly visible, except for a few shrapnel cuts. He had been in the ICU for two days, and the team hadn't managed to stabilize him enough to transport him to the military hospital in Landstuhl, Germany.

When I got there, he was on the ventilator. The team was doing everything possible to save his life. I read Psalm 23 from a Gideon Bible, then we all joined hands and I led a prayer. Usually, at that point, someone flips the switch, and we watch life leave the body. After a few minutes the patient flatlines, and the time of death is pronounced.

This young man's death hit me so profoundly that I wrote on the front page of the Bible and put it with his belongings in the Ziploc bag, which would accompany his body when it was sent to his parents. I wrote: *I want you to know that wonderful people worked hard to save your son. Hopefully, knowing we cared for him until the very last moment of his life will bring you comfort.*

When you're in a war zone, you focus on the few things you need and shut out everything else, because you can't handle it all.

When you're in a war zone, you focus on the few things you need and shut out everything else, because you can't handle it all.

People came into my office every day, asking, "How do I make it through this? I feel so overwhelmed." This was during the surge, the deadliest period of the war.

14

Over time, Balad Air Base became known as Mortaritaville, a play on the song "Margaritaville," as we were constantly attacked by rockets and mortar. In the seven months I served there, we experienced 208 such attacks. Personnel stationed there even had T-shirts printed that said, "I was deployed to Balad, Iraq, Mortaritaville."

Every time the alarms sounded, we dropped to the ground immediately because the blasts projected outward from the point of impact. The closer you got to the ground, the less likely you'd be wounded or killed by the explosion. It didn't matter if it was day or night. If you were in your vehicle, asleep in your bed, praying during a worship service, preaching, counseling someone, or walking from one place to another—when the alarm sounded, you dove to the ground.

We knew it could explode in as little as three seconds. If we were attacked by multiple rockets or mortars, it could take up to five minutes. After the attack was over, we could be down for thirty minutes or more before the area was checked, and the all-clear signal sounded.

Whenever I was face down, with my hands clasped over my neck, I thought, *this might be my time.* Most people pray that the ordinance is intercepted or falls somewhere else. That could be considered a selfish prayer, and it might be, but it was our reality. We didn't want someone else to be injured or killed—we were just so relieved to be alive. It's like when you come upon an auto accident and pray, "Thank you, God. If I had been here just a moment earlier, that might have been me." Being thankful you avoided trauma when others didn't doesn't make you a bad person. It makes you human.

> **Being thankful you avoided trauma when others didn't doesn't make you a bad person—it makes you human.**

I prayed that I would be kept safe. Some prayed that they had satisfied the requirements for salvation.

At the time, the predominant thought was *I've made it through many, many attacks, and my luck is about worn out.* When we got back to the States after deployment, during the mandatory transitional briefings, psychiatrists and psychologists told us, "Every attack affects you because you are at a perceived point of death." The majority of Christians I talked with told me that it kept them grounded spiritually because they were crying out and focusing on God.

I'd say, "Lord, I'm sorry if I did anything that requires me to ask for forgiveness." And I was as serious each and every time.

One Sunday, three intelligence agents were at the worship service, as they had been many times before when they weren't on a mission in the surrounding cities and towns. The next night they were sent on a mission to get intel. It turned out to be a setup. All three were killed.

I had just talked to those people. Now they were dead.

It was a difficult time to be a chaplain. Because no matter how much I hurt personally, I had a responsibility to help everyone else through the grieving process. I had a responsibility to hold a memorial service and a transfer ceremony when the bodies were placed in the aircraft for the flight back to Dover Air Force Base.

Surviving PTSD—in the truest sense, it's about accepting the small victories that come along each and every day. And it's important to remember that because our personalities and determination are all different, our journeys will not all be the same. We are not equipped to fight this battle alone, either. Successful endurance will require the help of other trusted individuals. And that's okay. Dependence on our family and friends is not failure. Reliance on behavioral health and medications is not a weakness.

There are wounds that never show on the body that are deeper and more hurtful than anything that bleeds.

Laurell K. Hamilton

Chapter 1

WHAT IS PTSD?

After experiencing or seeing a traumatic event, some people develop a mental health issue known as Post-Traumatic Stress Disorder, or PTSD. The traumatic event may be life-threatening, such as combat, a natural disaster, a car accident, or sexual assault. It's normal to feel afraid during and after a traumatic situation. The fear triggers a "fight-or-flight" response. This is how your body reacts as a way of protecting itself from possible harm, perceived or real.

In time, most people recover from this naturally. But people with PTSD don't begin to feel better with the passing of time. They feel stressed and frightened long after the trauma is over.

PTSD symptoms don't always begin right away. Some people might not experience symptoms until years after the traumatic event occurs. Symptoms might also come and go over time. They may come and go depending on a number of factors, such as stress, external surroundings, and overall well-being.

What is the Criteria for a PTSD Diagnosis?

- **Criterion A** (one required): The person was exposed to death, threatened death, actual or threatened serious injury, or actual or threatened sexual violence, in the following way(s): direct exposure, witnessing the trauma, indirect exposure to aversive details of the trauma, usually in the course of professional duties (e.g., first responders, medic, chaplains).

- **Criterion B** (one required): The traumatic event is persistently re-experienced, in the following way(s): unwanted upsetting memories, nightmares, flashbacks, emotional distress after exposure to traumatic reminders, physical reactivity after exposure to traumatic reminders.

- **Criterion C** (one required): The person avoids trauma-related stimuli after the trauma, in the following way(s): trauma-related thoughts or feelings, trauma-related reminders.

- **Criterion D** (two required): Negative thoughts or feelings began or worsened after the trauma, in the following way(s): inability to recall key features of the trauma, overly negative thoughts and assumptions about oneself or the world, exaggerated blame of self or others for causing the trauma's negative affect, decreased interest in activities, feeling isolated, difficulty experiencing positive effect.

- **Criterion E** (two required): Trauma-related arousal and reactivity began or worsened after the trauma, in the following way(s): irritability or aggression, risky or destructive behavior, hypervigilance, heightened startle reaction, difficulty concentrating, difficulty sleeping.

- **Criterion F** (required): Symptoms last for more than one month.

- **Criterion G** (required): Symptoms create distress or functional impairment (e.g., social, occupational).

- **Criterion H** (required): Symptoms are not due to medication, substance use, or other illness.

Categories of PTSD Symptoms

Symptoms of PTSD fall into four categories and can vary in severity. I identify the following symptoms in myself:

Intrusive Memories

Intrusion is the experience of intrusive thoughts, such as repeated, unwanted memories, distressing dreams, or flashbacks of the traumatic event. My thoughts and memories seem to have a mind of their own. When I say intrusion, I mean regularly having my train of thought attacked by a disturbing memory or thought I can't get out of my mind. In other words, the intrusions come back—again and again and again. Sometimes the intrusive thoughts even last for many days in a row.

Repeated, unwanted, disturbing memories that hijack your thoughts are an indication you could be suffering from PTSD.

I have very little control over whenever these intrusions will come on. What I do have *some* control over is whether they persist or remain a momentary thought. These thoughts and memories are like hearing a song or having someone mention a song, and all of a sudden, the music or lyrics are stuck in your head on a loop. As much as you want to get rid of the thought of the song and avoid repeating it inside, it doesn't seem to work.

When such intrusions or memories take place, they can linger in my mind for quite some time, and they are difficult to escape. We've all been there, perseverating something out of our control. The main difference with PTSD is these intrusive thoughts and memories are seldom good memories. They are most often bad memories. Troublesome thoughts. Things I wish I could unsee and unknow. They are lodged deep into my mind and heart. Something about them continues to intrude upon me without my control. It can be that, in some sense or another, I just haven't resolved the events of those thoughts. Much of what I have experienced seems unresolvable. I simply must learn to live with the thoughts and memories and hope to at some point gain more control over their hold on me.

Avoidance

Avoidance is dodging anything that reminds me of the traumatic events. I do this by avoiding people, places, activities, and situations that trigger my anxiety. I avoid thinking about the traumatic events that have transpired, and I often resist sharing about what happened or how I feel about it.

I have to live with the fact that avoidance is not always healthy. In fact, it can be counterproductive. One of the reasons I avoid is that I can't deal with whatever it is I'm avoiding. It could be classified as an escape mechanism. But wouldn't we rather avoid pain, whether it be physical or emotional? I think everyone tends to do that in their lives. No one chooses to dwell on the negative, destructive things having to do with life. It's so difficult to process and takes considerable energy to avoid.

Changes in Thinking and Mood

Third is changes in cognition and mood. I'm not able to remember the traumatic events' essential features. I often experience negative thoughts and distorted feelings concerning my actions, to the point where I believe bad things about myself. These beliefs can affect the very direction of my life. I also experience distorted thoughts about the cause or issues of traumatic memories. They lead to wrongly blaming myself, continuing fear, anger, guilt, or shame. I've even lost interest in some activities I previously enjoyed. I often feel disconnected or estranged from others. I find it difficult to experience positive sensation and have experienced a loss of happiness or satisfaction with things that once made me happy or content.

Changes in Physcial and Emotional Reactions

And finally, there are the anger-emotional states. Arousal and reactive symptoms include being irritable and having angry outbursts, being overly watchful of my surroundings, being easily startled, and having problems concentrating or sleeping.

Living on the edge. Having an edge. Though the two may seem somewhat the same, living on the edge and living *with* an edge are entirely two different things. Living on the edge is pushing a situation to the limit, taking risks, arousing ourselves by always taking one step more than most people. Living with an edge has more to do with our emotional state. Perhaps we can define it as having a chip on our shoulder, having something to prove, or wanting to make a point. What's clear about living with an edge is that it tends to push its way toward irritations, defensiveness, and anger. This edge, or edginess, puts us at odds with people and ourselves. Thus, we snap at people, challenge people…and it's miserable. I hate conflict. I want nothing more than to feel at peace with the people around me and at peace within myself.

Someone who suffers from PTSD often snaps at people they love with little or no provocation.

The Mayo Clinic definition of PTSD symptoms states that: "Post-traumatic stress disorder symptoms may start within one month of a traumatic event, but sometimes symptoms may not appear until years after the event. These symptoms cause significant problems in social or work situations and in relationships. They can also interfere with your ability to go about your normal daily tasks. PTSD symptoms are generally grouped into four types: intrusive memories, avoidance, negative changes in thinking and mood, and changes in physical and emotional reactions. Symptoms can vary over time or vary from person to person."[1]

I can also say with absolute certainty that I fall within the Mayo Clinic's definition for PTSD. Every word of the PTSD criteria, categories, and definition resonates deeply with me.

Endnote

1. Post-traumatic stress disorder (PTSD) - Symptoms and https://www.mayoclinic.org/diseases-conditions/post-traumatic-stress-disorder/symp-toms-causes/syc-20355967

If you have been diagnosed with PTSD, it is not a sign of weakness; rather, it is proof of your strength because you have survived.

HealthyPlace.com

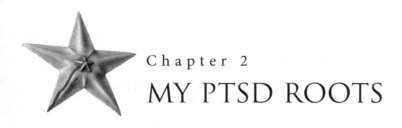

Chapter 2

MY PTSD ROOTS

E veryone's road to PTSD is unique. As I think back on *my* life, I believe the roots of PTSD were planted very early for me—even before my background as a military chaplain.

When I was seventeen years old, I began working on my hometown rescue squad. Most new members to the squad were able to ease into the work. While most rookies started with routine transfers or insignificant trips to the emergency room, this was not the case for me. I had no sort of "easing in" period. My very first call was anything but routine. It was a severe automobile accident. On our way to the scene, we learned a compact car had run up under the rear end of an 18-wheeler at high speed. The sheer force of the impact ripped off the top of the car. The other members of the rescue squad must have had an idea of what we were about to see, and while I knew it was going to be bad, I had no idea how bad it was actually going to be.

When we arrived, the scene of the car, barely recognizable now, had been carrying four teenage girls not much younger than myself. This gruesome visual hit me hard. All but one of the girls died instantly upon impact. Ill-equipped and completely unprepared for what we saw that day, I felt the wind knocked clear out of my chest. Had I not been trying to fit in with the squad, I would have retched everywhere.

To this day, decades later, thinking of this incomprehensible scene, impossible to forget or unsee, sends shivers down my spine. This experience did something to me. I was never the same. I was just a kid. I had no way of processing what I experienced that day. It was so awful that I considered resigning. This first experience with the rescue squad dug down deep roots of trauma within me that would lie in wait. I had no idea then that I would be no stranger to trauma. I hadn't even recovered when I experienced a second life-altering traumatic event.

I was just twenty-two years old when I experienced another traumatic event that would shape my life forever. My fiancée died tragically in a car accident just forty-six days before our wedding date. She was a schoolteacher and was getting her master's degree at night. After teaching all day, she had to drive two hours from Andalusia to Auburn University at Montgomery and take classes. She drove a Volkswagen Beetle.

Eyewitnesses observed that she seemed to have slowly drifted into the median. Then she jerked back and lost control of the car. It started flipping, and she was thrown out of the windshield. Seat belts were not required back then. Through all of this, God took care of her until the last minute of her life. It turned out that two of the people who saw the accident were nurses returning to Mobile after taking their state boards in Montgomery. They immediately stopped to provide physical care.

One of those nurses wanted us to know that they were there and comforted her in every way possible. The nurse told us she would nod her head and at times and would moan when she tried to respond to their questions but couldn't say any words. Just before she got to the point where she could not respond anymore, a minister ran up and asked if he could pray with her. She shook her head and somehow whispered the word "yes." That prayer was the last thing she experienced on this earth.

I had surrendered to preach when I was fifteen and had been preaching in numerous churches ever since. When she and I began dating, I told her I had no intention of becoming a full-time pastor. She always said, "God's calling you into full-time pastoral ministry, and you need to prepare for that." I knew from being around other full-time ministers the difficulties their families would experience. There are always people who are against the pastor's spouse and who are critical of the entire family. It's like living under a microscope.

I told her, "God's not calling me there. He's merely calling me to be a 'fill-in' preacher."

Her answer would always be, "You'll see. You'll find out one day, but I already know." She never wavered.

The day after her death, I was at her mother and father's house. Her mother and I went to her bedroom. We sat on her bed, which was surrounded by a large headboard filled with books. Her mother and I both knew she would wake up in the morning thirty minutes earlier than she needed and read. After she had read for thirty minutes, she would place the opened book face-down. As her mother and I sat there on her bed and cried together, her mother picked up the book that she had been reading the previous morning. She was about halfway through this particular book. When her mother saw it, she just came apart. She dropped it, I picked it up and read the title—*The Pastor's Wife*.

She had believed in and was preparing for my ministry—even if I wasn't. I ended up dedicating my ministry to her faithful belief that this was God's plan for my life. I went back to school and finished my ministry degree.

Our pastor thought it would be a good idea to be re-licensed the day after our scheduled wedding date. He said, "I want to relicense you in the worship service. And I want you to preach that morning." Sadly, I didn't share his conviction.

On the day that would have been our wedding date, I still had so much bitterness in my heart. I went to see her mother and her father. They had a pond out back, so I just went out by myself and literally yelled at God as loudly as I could.

"She loved You. I love You and have given my life to serve You, and You haven't taken this bitterness away. I have to get up and preach and be licensed again tomorrow. If You don't take away this feeling by the time I get into the pulpit, I'll tell everyone You don't deserve my love. You put me in this place, and You're allowing me to continue to feel this terrible pain. If I still feel all this pain tomorrow, I'll curse You from the pulpit." I was very serious about that, and I thought about the things I would say. Instead of preaching a sermon, I would intentionally curse God and walk out.

During Sunday school the following day, our pastor gave me his office and said, "Just sit down by yourself and get your head together." I was preparing to preach the message. The problem was my bitterness was still there. Crying out to the Lord had done nothing to relieve my pain. When the worship service began, the bitterness was still there, and in my head, I thought, *Truly, Lord, I see you don't care. You don't love me enough to take away the pain and I'm going to follow through with my threat.*

The amazing thing about God is through all that bitterness, He knew the depths of my heart—not merely my overwhelming emotions. Through all my heartbreak, pain, suffering and bitterness, He reached down to me.

God knew the depths of my heart. Through all my heartbreak, pain, suffering and bitterness, He reached down to me.

As I walked toward the pulpit, I still felt all the pain, and I was ready to start proclaiming what I had threatened. Then I stood behind the pulpit. In an instant, all bitterness washed away. I just felt normal. Like I hadn't felt in weeks. I preached the sermon that I had prepared. Afterward, I was

31

able to say, "Never in my life will I doubt Your love again. I cursed at You. I shouted at You. Yet You saw beyond my hurt and pain and still loved me."

Although, the pain and bitterness returned a few hours later, God had taken it away long enough for Him to instill a simple truth. He didn't take me completely out of my pain. I had to go through grief just like everyone else, but He wanted me to know He still loved me—despite my feelings.

If I'm completely honest about my PTSD, I'm sure much of it goes all the way back to losing her. I was only twenty-two years old. The trauma of losing her was undeniable. I was in immense pain even though I knew God loved me.

Every morning I prayed: "Lord, please, take me today. I want to be with her. I know that I'm saved. I have no doubt. I know You love me. Go ahead and take me today, so I can be with her."

A year earlier I had been a city police officer. One day I was in so much pain that I took my Colt Trooper Mark 3, 357 magnum service revolver and put it up to my head. As awful as it may have been, the thought that came to my mind was, *I believe I'll go to heaven, but what if I'm wrong? What if it wasn't true? I can't take my life and possibly end up in hell.* That thought saved my life.

Since the day of the accident, I had woken up every morning, and the first words that always came out of my mouth were, "Lord, I'm ready to go. Take me today. Take me out of this pain." I didn't even have to think about it. It was automatically the first thing in my mind.

Then—out of nowhere—one day, for no apparent reason, I woke up, and the first thing that came out of my mouth was, "Thank You for giving me another day. I pray I can influence the lives of others. Use me. I am so blessed." It was like a switch had flipped. Where there was no hope for happiness, there was now hope.

I carried on from that day with my mission to be in ministry. I had no idea then where that would lead me in the years and decades to come. Over the course of the next three decades, I would deploy a total of five times. From Norway to Haiti, South Korea, Iraq, and finally Afghanistan.

I had no idea all those years ago all that I would experience as a minister and chaplain. How could I have known? I was just a kid. And no one truly understands what they are getting into until they are right in the middle of it—especially in war.

... PTSD (results from) ... a very traumatic event. And actually, there is evidence that brain chemistry changes during this event in certain individuals where it's imprinted indelibly forever and there's an emotion associated with this which triggers the condition.

Dale Archer

Chapter 3

CAREGIVING AND PTSD

P TSD is the most common manifestation of emotional disorders in caregivers. The ministry and faith chaplains use to help others makes it even harder to address. A chaplain's role, rank, and knowledge can work against identifying disorder in their own lives. Chaplains are beacons of hope for believers and non-believers, the churched and the unchurched, the saved and the lost. Chaplains can be found in war zones comforting troops, unsure whether they will live through the day or see their families again. They minister to families and medical staff in emergency rooms where life hangs in the balance. Chaplains regularly deliver death notifications to loved ones who immediately need the comfort of someone who cares. They work with first responders in the police, fire or rescue departments to help them process the tragedies they witness.

In times of crisis, chaplains become visible reminders of God.

The opportunities for chaplaincy ministry are unlimited. Chaplains accept a special charge, knowing that it will require separation from their families, being placed in harm's way, and witnessing and sharing the pain of those suffering under their care. Chaplains are caregivers who have answered the Great Commission's call to go forth and minister to the ends of the earth.

Over time, I learned how to reduce my mountain of repressed trauma. But years back, each time I was deployed, I didn't have strategies in place to push back on that mountain—and the stockpile of trauma I was carrying deep within grew bigger and bigger. I saw more, counseled more, heard more—and while my experiences were deeply meaningful, I couldn't deny that I felt more and more fear over my own safety, as the magnitude of injuries and casualties increased exponentially in my final locations, Iraq and Afghanistan.

So why did I continue with the job and even love my deployments? Because ministry in a war zone is exhilarating, and I love helping people, especially in their direst need. I have sat beside grief for all of my adult life, and I wouldn't have it any other way. It is and always will be my calling. I struggle to even admit how much it all has affected me. I downplay it. I internalize it. But I know that doesn't help the next person who is struggling with PTSD to find a lifeboat. It is possible to at the same time love what you are doing—to feel completely called— and to feel the weight of crisis, loss, and grief like a heavy load you can't set down.

Chaplains and Mental Health

The mental health of chaplains as it relates to PTSD is unique. I recently saw a news segment on chaplains working in the

COVID-19 environment that noted chaplains are now working on the frontlines of faith-based ministry. The truth is, chaplains have always been on the front lines of ministry. Often, they are the only visible reminder of the Holy. Whether in military, healthcare, law enforcement, or institutional environments, chaplains minister as spiritual first-responders. Many times, they are putting their own lives at risk.

Mental health issues are an unavoidable part of chaplaincy ministry. The main thrust of chaplaincy is to minister to people during the worst times of their lives. Most often, chaplains are present during the crisis or very soon after. Those affected are emotionally charged or in a state of shock. It's a time when people are most vulnerable. People remember those moments throughout their lives. Often the spiritual care they receive from a chaplain endears them to the ministry forever. No more significant impact can be made on a person's life than supporting them in a crisis. Many attribute a significant element in their healing to that interaction with faith.

Being a crisis chaplain means being bombarded with negative emotions—anger, fear, and grief—and for many, it's a recipe for mental health issues. A chaplain's mission is to provide comfort, hope, and stability in a time of crisis. With so many interactions in such a short period, the chaplain has no time to process his personal grief, which often results in unresolved emotional issues. His commitment to himself is to draw strength from God as he navigates one crisis at a time, but this does not mean there is not a cost.

I have experienced so much vicarious pain and suffering that at some point it all became my own. Like a tornado, my own pain and the atrocities I have witnessed mixed with the pain and atrocities of thousands of others has torn through my heart and mind, leaving a deep path of pain and trauma. At the end of a tornado, when everything becomes eerily still, what once stood tall and strong is nothing but a pile of scraps—unrecognizable shadows of what once was. The same is true for emotional upheaval and turmoil. What was once strong and resolved is now broken and damaged beyond full repair. I am filled with scars, these well-worn paths of pain and sorrow. I carry the scars of others atop my own deep unhealed wounds.

Being a sensitive and deeply feeling person makes me a better chaplain, but I now understand that those parts of myself make me more susceptible to mental health issues—specifically PTSD.

Crisis faith intervention is an inevitable part of every day for military chaplains serving in a war zone. They fear for those they are called to serve, but they also fear for their own lives, which undoubtedly intensifies the impact on their own mental health. In general, ministers have great sympathy and empathy for those to whom they minister. I am no exception. Continuing to carry the pain of others is emotionally tiring, and the extra load chaplains carry in dealing with their own anxiety, grief, depression, and fear makes them even more susceptible to emotional disorders.

I have felt and still feel the emotional exhaustion of carrying the pain of those to whom I have ministered. I recall every scene—the most gruesome sights you can imagine. I recall every story—men and women breaking open under the weight of war. Each and every interaction is branded on my heart and mind.

Vicarious grief, vicarious pain, vicarious trauma in addition to my own grief, pain and trauma set the awful foundation for the PTSD I live with now.

During times of deployment, I was often the highest ranking chaplain. This meant I had no one to go to with my own pain. I had no one to talk with when the weight of it all was bearing down on me. I turned to God and my faith during these times. I prayed. I sought wisdom and strength from God. Although God got me through my most trying times, it set up a dynamic of feeling like I did not need to seek out help.

Before being diagnosed with PTSD, I didn't want to get help because I didn't think there was anything wrong with me. I could readily see the effects and identify the disorder in other people, while I had a hard time allowing myself to see those same effects in my life. I exhibited all the criteria for PTSD but was still fighting the reality of what that meant for me. I know the data, yet I struggled—still struggle—to identify fully with the impact of PTSD.

Before being diagnosed with PTSD, I didn't want to get help because I didn't think there was anything wrong with me.

A recent survey conducted by the Evangelical Chaplains Commission reported the following:

- 22% of chaplains have been diagnosed with Post Traumatic Stress Disorder.

- 26% have not been diagnosed, but believe they have PTSD.

- 45% have experienced anxiety beyond normal levels.

- 7% are currently taking antidepressants, anti-anxiety, or psychotropic drugs.

- 26% have sought help for a mental disorder during their chaplaincy career.

- 15% have considered or attempted suicide during their chaplaincy career.

We must address these statistics and overcome the obstacles to seeking help. In medical circles, it's summed up as "Physician, heal thyself." We assume that as examples of strong faith, we can protect ourselves. Surely, if I can identify and help others, teaching coping mechanisms for combating PTSD, then I must be okay. The higher in rank we go, the less we are willing to admit what we perceive as weakness. Our conclusions are based on faulty reasoning and keeps many from seeking the help they need.

The higher in rank we go, the less we are willing to admit what we perceive as weakness.

PTSD and Faith

I hope to destigmatize the conversations surrounding PTSD—especially as it relates to faith. We know that by sharing our circumstances, we give others the opportunity to share theirs as well. There are always roadblocks to sharing—shame, pride, fear, guilt—and faith. Faith may seem an odd roadblock at first glance, but it is real and presents a formidable challenge to those suffering with PTSD.

It is challenging to be a person of faith when dealing with an ailment or circumstance that seems to take more and more control of your life with every passing day. We learn early on in our faith journeys that God alone is in control of our lives. There is a notion that if I pray harder, trust God more, or surrender all to God, all pain should cease. While I know with my mind that this is not the way God works, my heart has a harder time understanding why I have yet to feel any relief from my condition. As a person of deep abiding faith, I seek Him daily. I pray to be healed. I cry out to him to answer me and take my suffering away. His answer thus far has been "no." This is difficult to swallow. I know He loves me. I know His plans for me are good. I just don't understand why He hasn't offered the littlest bit of relief. I may never understand. This challenges me and my faith. I have to fight harder to stay close to God. I have to rely on what I know of His character and how He works in people's lives.

I've been asked hundreds if not thousands of times over the years how people without faith in God make it through life's tragedies and trauma. You would think the answer would be simple. The answer

41

I usually give people is this: "It's actually easier for those without faith." That may sound ridiculous since faith can be such a positive influence when people are suffering from PTSD. But in many ways, this unresolved pain may be easier for people of no faith at all. In this, they are able to blame God for all they have been through and all they are feeling. Placing the blame on God makes it easier to bear somehow—the weight of it all feels a bit lighter. They don't have to take responsibility for anything. It's God's fault. If He were a loving God, then He wouldn't make good people suffer. Diverting their pain and anger onto God offers some relief for those with no faith in Him.

I am a man of great faith, but I still struggle to understand what God is doing with me and this experience. There was a time in my life that I believed one's faith should be able to save a person from anything. I know better now. I am more mature. Even still, there's not a day that goes by that I don't beg Him to take this from me.

I am tired. I am sick of the lies. I am sick of pretending. I am sick of hiding behind the mask of "I'm fine."

Please hear my heart. I would be a chaplain all over again to help the men and women I have been in service to. Every single bit of it. I would sit bedside for days. I would put myself in harm's way. I would hold the hands of every single hurting person. This complicates people's—and my own—understanding of my PTSD. I would never want to wave a magic wand and take it all away. Those years were many of the most life-giving and rewarding of my chaplaincy. But the cumulative impact of trauma has a way of catching up with a person.

I am not fine. I am a work in progress. I am actively working on permitting myself to feel the effects of my PTSD. I seek daily to allow myself grace and acceptance of that which I cannot control. My prayer is that many others suffering with PTSD will allow themselves the same grace and permission. This is where the healing begins.

PTSD is not evidence that you were
abandoned or betrayed by God.
He is there. With you in the darkness.
Beside you in the valley.
His compassion is tender and real. Even
when it is beyond your comprehension,
know this: God is at work.

Wendy K. Walters

Chapter 4

MY DIAGNOSIS AND JOURNEY THROUGH THE STAGES OF GRIEF

In the two and a half years since I'd come back from Iraq, my wife and daughter kept telling me that I hadn't been myself. They kept saying they thought I had PTSD.

Though they begged me to get help, I didn't want to. I believed they were being unreasonable.

I was a chaplain. I had a background in marriage and family therapy. I held a master's in psychology and counseling. Signs of traumatic stress and coping techniques were no strangers to me. If something was wrong with me, I was sure I'd know. But after continued encouragement, to put my wife and daughter at ease, I made an appointment with a psychologist at Defense Stress Management for a PTSD diagnosis. (I didn't tell my wife and daughter I was going, or even that I'd made the appointment—I just planned to see the psychologist and return home with the good news that I was okay.)

Diagnosis

On the day of the appointment, the psychologist explained how the diagnostic process worked. The patient was required to attend three sessions to answer assessment questions, and then a diagnosis would be made. That was all. When the psychologist asked if I was willing to do that, I said sure. I even told him that I'd be a very easygoing patient: I wouldn't lie or hold back. Sure, I'd hoped we would get the process over with in one visit, but if a diagnosis required three visits, I could do that. No problem.

During that first session, nothing seemed out of the ordinary. I felt comfortable answering his assessment questions, and at the end of the hour he said, "That's all for today."

Flippantly, I replied, "One down and two to go."

The psychologist then looked me in the eye. "Chaplain," he said, "we always see a patient for three visits before diagnosing PTSD. This is the first time I've ever done this, but I'm recommending you be diagnosed with PTSD now. It's that apparent."

A chill ran through my body.

"I don't need any further visits to be sure," he continued. "In your case, I'll talk with the psychiatrist who's been assigned to you. He'll meet with you in the next few days and officially diagnose you with Post-Traumatic Stress Disorder."

People in my life know that I'm never at a loss for words. But there I was...speechless! I was baffled.

It took a minute for me to gain my composure. When I did, I challenged his diagnosis. But after some back and forth, it became evident that the psychologist wasn't going to change what he planned to put in his report.

The next couple of days were a whirlwind. Focusing at work was impossible; I couldn't get what the psychologist had said off my mind. *"It's that apparent."*

Still, I didn't tell my wife or daughter about the appointment or what happened. My rationale was that the psychiatrist would surely come to the opposite conclusion, and then all of this would be over.

But when I met with the psychiatrist, that's not what happened. In fact, he echoed the psychologist's thoughts.

He said he had no doubt I had Post-Traumatic Stress Disorder.

That's when hot tears fell down my face. His words slammed into me, hitting me hard, like I had just run into a wall. My initial reaction was blurting the first words that came out of my mouth:

"Are you *kidding* me?"

Of course, that statement was mostly rhetorical. Deep within, I knew the psychiatrist must be serious. I didn't want him to be right, but I realized he was the authority, the doctor.

"No," he said, cementing the diagnosis. It was real now.

I walked out of the office in a daze. Time stood eerily still. So many thoughts raced through my mind. A convergence of shock, fear, shame, and guilt overwhelmed me—but the one feeling I didn't have inside me was acceptance.

I didn't know it at the time, but this was the definitive moment when my ongoing battle with PTSD began. I had already been in denial for two and a half years prior to this day. It felt like two immovable objects had come into hard contact. Reality had collided with a realization I was not ready to admit. Though I had counseled people with PTSD for years, I didn't expect it to happen to me, and that made me feel out of control—probably more so than I'd ever felt in my life.

I didn't have a plan past talking with my wife. So when I got home, I sat down with Cherri and told her I had sought help and was in fact suffering with PTSD. She must have had some of the typical reactions that anyone living with a spouse suffering with PTSD would have. It was such a shocking, sobering event that I can't even recall her initial reaction.

Little did I know how much my life would change after that.

After the diagnosis, I knew I couldn't hide anymore—from others or myself. (Though no one outside my family had ever brought up the topic of PTSD with me, I'm sure people must have thought something was wrong.) The problem was I was trained to help others, but I had no idea what I needed to do to help myself. If this were happening to a friend, a colleague, a soldier, I would know exactly what to say. I would immediately have a plan in mind to help them through this diagnosis. But when it came to me, I was a ship lost at sea.

In 1969, Elisabeth Kübler-Ross introduced the world to a new concept about working through grief. She reasoned that when a person faces loss after the death of someone they care for, there are distinct stages of grieving: denial, anger, bargaining, depression, and acceptance.

Those suffering from PTSD also go through loss. Not the loss of a loved one's life, but the loss of parts of who they were before the PTSD. When the roots of my PTSD set in—and especially after the diagnosis—I definitely was not the man I was before. Though I care very deeply for people, my actions and reactions didn't show evidence of a caring, loving individual. I'd been replaced by someone I didn't want to be or even knew anymore.

> **Though I care very deeply for people, my actions and reactions didn't show evidence of a caring, loving individual.**

I will attempt to translate the grief of loss into my experiences with my affliction.

Denial

Grief begins with denial. When we get the news that someone has died, we hesitate to fully grasp such a shocking thought. "They're not really gone," we think. Or we think, "No, this isn't possible." Denying the truth is a way for us to cope with the loss.

Many people who are diagnosed with PTSD don't readily accept the diagnosis. When it becomes abundantly clear that something is not right—when we can no longer ignore our overt symptoms—we deny them, questioning the symptoms and whether they're significant enough to deserve a PTSD diagnosis.

In the two and a half years before I sought help and was diagnosed, I knew and my loved ones knew that I wasn't happy. I was thankful that I'd made it back from Iraq alive and grateful for everything in my life that I'd taken for granted previously, but that didn't change how my deployment affected me. Interestingly, I was very aware of my PTSD symptoms because my training and counseling made me keenly aware of such signs. However, it was difficult to recognize my own symptoms as legitimate.

Even when my symptoms affected my everyday life and those around me, I ignored them with fairly good success. I didn't dwell on them. I quickly integrated them into my life under the guise of "this is just how things are now."

Anger

When you lose someone, anger is a normal follow-up response to denial.

But where does anger fit into a PTSD diagnosis? Does the person feel anger toward the diagnosis itself? Is their anger directed at the doctor who diagnosed it? Self-directed? Or do they feel angry at the whole situation?

For me, it was all of the above. Though the sharpest anger was directed inward.

The diagnosis delivered an emotional blow to my body. A near physical punch to the gut. It caused immediate, intense pain. When we know we're about to get punched, we instinctively tense our abdominal muscles to protect us from the blow. But when our guard is down and we don't get the chance to react, it knocks the breath out of us. Our brains get rattled. Too many thoughts and ideas immediately vie for attention. With those emotions crisscrossing together in a web of uncertainty, it makes sense that I would get angry.

Bargaining

Losing someone can bring you to your knees—you might feel like you'll do anything, strike any deal, to get that person back. And the same may be true for someone processing a PTSD diagnosis.

Dealing is my kind of game. My philosophy has always been that you won't get anything if you don't ask. So bargaining is just a part of who I am. When it comes to my PTSD, the deals I pleaded for were typically made with God because I am a man of faith.

"God," I'd say, "If you'll just take this from me, I'll ... "

"Give me one more chance to be better. I promise to do ... or not do ..."

Many times I have said the words, "I'll do anything for you, God," hoping He would take the pain of my diagnosis away.

You can imagine that I did a great deal of bargaining in the early stages of my PTSD.

Depression

When you face the loss of a loved one head on—after denying, seething, and bargaining—it's common to feel depressed. Depression is different from being unhappy. It's more intense. It lasts longer and has a prolonged negative impact on our lives.

People who get diagnosed with PTSD might fall into depression as well. (People with PTSD are three to five times more likely to be depressed than those who don't have PTSD.) Among the signs and symptoms connecting PTSD to depression are loss of interest or pleasure, difficulty sleeping, fatigue or restlessness, thoughts of dying or suicide, unwanted memories, flashbacks, avoidance of trauma triggers, feelings of isolation, negative thoughts and emotions, irritability, and hypervigilance.

Acceptance

For those who have lost—and for those with PTSD—acceptance is not necessarily a moment in time. Rather, it's a progression. It would be much easier to deal with our disorder if it were neatly packaged as a one-and-done proposition. Still, acceptance is an important goal to strive for so we can heal from the emotional effects of trauma.

Accepting PTSD is like taking baby steps. The progression may be unsteady—often, the progress is so minute that we're not even aware of it—but at some point it does bring relief.

People who experience traumatic injuries or diseases usually don't recognize their strength and healing as much as those around them do. I've known people who were making remarkable progress in their healing, but felt like they weren't getting better. They fought every day with conditioning and therapy, only to feel they were progressing too slowly and/or not at all. Much the same can be said about accepting PTSD. It happens slowly and without much satisfaction.

I know that PTSD affects me in a similar way. I'm so aware of just how much is "wrong" with me that each step forward seems insignificant compared to how far I need to go.

I don't like many things about myself now. I am content, but not joyous. Part of dealing with PTSD is accepting who you are, although you are no longer the person you once were. I fought that. I didn't want to admit that I was emotionally and socially different now.

Acceptance is still a challenge for me. It's always one step forward, two steps back. It's a dance that I've grown accustomed to. I've accepted the dance but still have a hard time simply accepting the diagnosis. Numerous times, my psychiatrist wrote in his notes, "The patient will not give himself permission to have PTSD." My rationale was that my experiences had not been nearly as bad as so many others, and as far as I knew, most of *them* didn't have a problem.

Twelve years later, I'm still working on acceptance. I still have a hard time believing I have PTSD. I suspect I always will.

Part of dealing with PTSD is accepting who you are, although you are no longer the person you once were.

Steve West

Chapter 5

ANXIETY

A nxiety can best be defined as a feeling of fear, dread, and uneasiness. I live with anxiety. It affects me every day of my life at various levels. It causes me to feel restless and tense, and have a rapid heartbeat. It can be a normal reaction to stress. I might feel anxious when facing a difficult problem at work, or before making an important decision. It can even help me to cope. With PTSD the fear is not temporary and can be overwhelming. While always lurking, it's not a continuous feeling. Sometimes I get to the point that it's there, but it's manageable. There are times when I don't think about it as much. Being anxious doesn't completely shut me down usually, but it does in the worst times. It's hold on me depends a lot on what I'm thinking. I am always trying to find some way to control it if I can.

An example of what can affect me is as follows: My heart is beating so hard that I feel it in my chest and in my ears. My heart rate is up—so high that I feel dizzy and short of breath. Even though I am sitting completely still, I have shakiness going on inside of me, and it's all over my body—from head to toe, down my arms, and out of my fingertips. Anxiety shaking is like shivering, only on the inside. We can only stop shivering by getting warm. No matter how much we want it to stop, we cannot control it. I have to focus on something else. Sometimes, just like today, it's causing me to physically shake on the outside. My arms and hands are the places that I can see the most, especially when the anxiety first sets in. Much of the anxiety has to do with the part of me that is deep in denial despite living with it every single day of my life. Accepting anxiety as your new normal is almost impossible. A PTSD diagnosis helps you understand your symptoms, but it's still unfathomable that this is happening to you. You can't think rationally about your PTSD when you are neck deep in symptoms. You are in survival mode—just fighting to keep from drowning.

A PTSD diagnosis helps you understand your symptoms, but it's still unfathomable that this is happening to you.

Goosebumps accompany my anxiety. I haven't quite figured out this symptom. Perhaps my outside body is reacting to the chaos within. It feels as if the anxiety is physically trying to leave my body through any way possible. It's not a particularly distressing symptom like many of the others. The goosebumps are more of a red flag—a warning sign—that I am stressed and the situation could escalate quickly. My breathing is highly pronounced and seems to be in line with the racing of my heartbeat. I can feel my heart pounding, incessantly invading my body. I want to wrap my hands around it and induce a calming effect. It's a physical feeling without an escape. In people with situational or circumstantial anxiety, there are times when your attention is drawn to the pronounced beating heart. Whereas in the case of anxiety related to PTSD, it's to a point where the beating can feel like your heart might be coming out of your chest.

I've come to realize that even before I feel my heart pounding, I will notice I've got my jaw clenched and it's there I realize that I am feeling out of sorts. Jaw clenching is clearly present during times of high anxiety. When I notice how tight the pressure is on my teeth from the clenching, I have to consciously tell myself to relax my jaw. It's a sign to me that I'm stressed, and the anxiety is building. This inner dialogue can go on and on numerous times during the anxiety as I fight to keep from clenching. The incessant gives way to aching pain.

Awareness and Managing My Anxiety

There are some ways I have found that help me to drown out everything and get a handle on the anxiety. Putting on headphones and playing music can be very helpful. I just close my eyes and simply listen. There are many, many ways to ease stress. When I'm in the throes of anxiety, headphones and music are my great allies. Another thing that helps is TV. If I can get myself to watch a show or movie, the other things begin to fade away. It's because I'm focusing on something active at that moment that is not threatening to me. I don't have to think about whatever has me so anxious. I try to separate myself from whatever is causing the stress and the ensuing anxiety.

Typically, the stress that bothers me most is when I'm frustrated—when I'm arguing with someone, or they're adverse. When someone criticizes me or wants to know why I did something a certain way, I immediately begin to feel the stress and anxiety rise. In the last couple of years, I've noticed it bothers me more and more. The occurrences have grown more common. Now, I find myself intentionally avoiding these situations. I want to shut it down. I don't want to deal with the conflict at all.

Interestingly, I'm now just beginning to make the distinction between my attacks and conflict. I really try to avoid conflict any way that I can, especially with my wife. There are many times that I won't say anything because I know it will lead to heightened tensions. That heightening of tension brings with it anxiety, shaking inside, and an immediate desire to separate me from the conflict. It's that flight to try to get my head back together and not feel the anxiety.

The internal shaking that comes from anxiety feels like it wants to come out of my skin, and begin shaking my body physically instead of just emotionally. Sometimes I find myself lifting my arm, and holding out my hand to see if the shakiness has moved to an outside physical tremor. When I get to this point I can't hone in on anything but the feelings. I find it very difficult to think about other things. It takes over just that much, and that's when I get quiet. I'm trying to figure out one what happened when I'm not sure what happened. Quickly, it turns to worry and I start to worry about how I'm going to solve whatever it is or figure out what in the world triggered me. I'm pacing now back and forth in my office. It's located upstairs in my home, so I don't have to worry about anyone seeing me doing this and wondering why.

As long as I can remember I've been a pacer. If I'm talking to someone on the phone and I'm not sitting at my desk, I'll just pace and look out the window. It doesn't have anything to do with anxiety. The anxiety exacerbates it. It is a heightening of what I'm feeling. I'm so tired of this. It's hard to have these kinds of thoughts.

I know all too well what conflict does to me. Interestingly, when the conflict is with someone you're close to, the stress, frustration, and anxiety just seem to be multiplied. When this happens, I go into avoidance mode. I stop engaging. I shut down. To my wife this must feel as though I am dismissing her or ignoring her. This is upsetting to us both, but this is just one of the many fallouts of living with PTSD.

Of course, there are many different things that trigger the anxiety, but conflict and feeling overwhelmed really take hold of me. At this moment, while I'm writing this section, I'm beginning to feel the anxiety building in me. I feel the shaking and shivering starting inside. The shivering is so hard to describe and even harder for people to understand. The shivers race down my spine and down and out my hands, legs, and feet. It's like trapped air or energy that has nowhere else to go, so it just flutters and wreaks havoc throughout the body. To say it is uncomfortable and unsettling would be a vast understatement. It is the epitome of anxiety and the realization of its presence compounds the anxiety even more. It is a never ending loop of symptoms—a snowball effect of which I have zero control.

My quickening heartbeat is now very pronounced and invading. Just trying to describe it on paper or by recording it causes tension to start building up. I think that's because PTSD, in the way that only it can, begins to take hold. There are some days where I can do things normally, but when I am anxiety-ridden, it tends to last all day. As strange as it might be, this anxiety is caused by situations in the present. Quite often, I don't have any idea what's causing me to feel anxiety in myself. There is no rhyme or reason to it. Some days I can manage, and some days it's absolute misery from the time I wake up until the time I go to bed. There is no magic button to push or magic pill to swallow that will take it all away. Regrettably, anxiety is something I live with every day. The same way another person may be living with diabetes or any other health condition that may require daily attention and maintenance.

Normal Anxiety vs. Anxiety from PTSD

It's important to understand that this is not your average, everyday anxiety. We can be anxious about something good or something we're looking forward to taking place. Situational anxiety is far different from anxiety related to PTSD. Normal anxiety caused by things like preparing to give a speech or gearing up for a big event is transient. It comes and then after the event; it goes. Not so with anxiety related to PTSD. Not for me at least. It comes, but it never goes. It's always with me. This is one of the most difficult things to explain to people who have not walked my same path. My anxiety has no cause—no specific cause at least. I know it all goes back to deployment, but there is no single event that I can pinpoint.

My anxiety can start up anytime, anywhere, and for any reason. You have to understand that PTSD changes you. You don't go back to being the same person you were before. In most cases, it means that the PTSD altered the way you process things or even your outlook. It also changes your personality, and just like with anything, the worse your PTSD is, the more it changes you. The more you feel changed by something out of your control, the more your mind begins to spin— adding even more anxiety to your already full plate.

Negative self-talk intensifies my anxiety. I know how easy it is for our thoughts to deteriorate. Even though I know how this snowballing of negative self-talk works, it still often takes a hold on me. It starts with a thought and soon after self-doubt, fear or anger—all three and many more feelings and emotions—set in depending on the situation ahead of me. Once the feelings begin to take root, before long I am saying to myself, "There is no way I can do this." "This will never work." The mind is only capable of one thought at a time.

After a traumatic experience, the human system of self-preservation seems to go onto permanent alert, as if the danger might return at any moment.

Judith Lewis Herman

Chapter 6
ANGER

Though anger is one of the middle stages of grief, for those with PTSD, it's a particularly complex emotion that we may find ourselves dipping back into again and again. It's a dance, much like the road to acceptance.

Our relationship with anger can be frightening since anger is not a feeling or emotion that most people are comfortable with. And while on the surface, anger might seem like it explodes out of nowhere, there's usually a root to anger: anxiety. For me, anxiety is a feeling of fear, dread, and uneasiness, usually over not being in control of my diagnosis.

The anxiety in my life isn't every moment. Sometimes it's manageable. In fact, sometimes I don't think about it that much altogether.

But it's always lurking.

Stoked by an argument, or criticism, or a problem at work—or something else entirely—anxiety manifests itself in a physical way for me. Rapid heart rate, dizziness, shortness of breath, and the internal shaking I described in the last chapter.

Other symptoms accompany my anxiety: goosebumps, jaw-clenching, pacing. Perhaps the goosebumps are a reaction that my outside body has to the chaos within me. It's as if the anxiety is physically trying to leave my body through any way possible.

Once the anxiety kicks in, it can turn into stress, then frustration, and then—finally—anger. For me the anger sits just below the surface. It's invisible until my anxiety escalates, and I reach a point where I can no longer deny it or hide it. Before that happens, I usually go into avoidance mode. I stop engaging. I shut down.

My anger sits just below the surface, invisible until my anxiety escalates, and I reach a point where I can no longer deny it or hide it.

I don't like feeling this way. Like I am like a red-hot exposed nerve just waiting to snap. It is against my better nature. I love people. I love communicating and sharing. I am angry at my anger, and that this seems to be my new normal. I am angry that PTSD has stolen so much from me—that it has irrevocably altered the very essence of my being—and that feeling makes those moments when my anxiety spills into anger even worse.

Normal Frustration Triggers Angry Overreactions

Once, when I was stationed at the Pentagon, my wife and I went to the commissary at Bolling Air Force Base for groceries. Afterward, we decided to go to the base exchange across the parking lot and have dinner at the food court, where we'd have a choice of five or six fast-food restaurants.

When we walked in, I could tell that they were doing construction in the food court area. It turned out that they were remodeling the area, and I noticed they had several things going on work-wise at the beverage station. I decided to get a sandwich from the sub shop. When I told the cashier that I wanted a large fountain drink, she said, "All we have right now are bottled drinks." I remember thinking, "They're charging me the same price for a bottled drink that I'd pay for a larger fountain drink, and I could have all the refills I wanted for free."

I wasn't aware that what happened next was out of line, but when I thought about it a few days later, I was horrified. The cashier told me that the first thing I did was lash out.

"The only thing you have is *bottled drinks*?" I said, agitated. "Why don't they have something set up for the fountain while they're working?"

My response was ridiculous. None of this was the cashier's fault. But at the time, I thought I was reacting reasonably. Understand that this was not isolated instance.

My wife, Cherri, was embarrassed. She tried to get me to keep moving, which I finally did. At that moment, I thought what I was doing was okay. It didn't even dawn on me that my behavior was ugly, although it was apparent to everybody else. That wasn't a good night. For days, my wife didn't want to talk to me. She didn't even want to be with me. She was living through this type of behavior over and over again.

What's interesting is that if I had seen somebody else behave that way, I would have been agitated, too—I probably would have even said something.

Sometimes I think about that moment. And frequently I ask myself why anger was my go-to reaction. It's certainly not the way I want to respond to life's challenges.

Thankfully, through the years I have found ways to help me drown out everything and get a handle on my anxiety before it morphs into anger. When I'm in the throes of anxiety, headphones and music are my great allies: I turn on a relaxing tune, close my eyes, and simply listen. Watching TV is another helpful distraction. As I focus on a show or movie, the stress I'm experiencing begins to fade away.

Anger is natural in our emotional response to trauma. It's at the center of the survival response in people. It's often the way we cope with life's stresses; it gives us the energy to keep going in the face of peril. But for someone living with PTSD, anger is an unrelenting presence. It can create divides in our relationships with those we love the most. And I'm constantly working to understand and manage that presence.

There's a scene in *Forrest Gump* that reminds me of my experience with anger and PTSD. Jenny has returned to her home after her abusive father's funeral. The family home has become an unlivable shell, abandoned for years. Standing in front of the house, she starts thinking back on memories of the abuse she endured growing up. Anger swells inside and turns to rage. She begins to throw rocks at the house forcefully and finally falls to the ground in defeat.

As the scene ends, Forrest says, "Sometimes there just aren't enough rocks."

**Intense emotions are common with
complex trauma survivors. Learning
to manage and regulate emotions
is vital in being able to manage all
the other (PTSD) symptoms.**

Lily Hope Lucario

Chapter 7

THE SCIENCE OF PTSD

S cience isn't something I associate with PTSD. As a matter of fact, I consider PTSD the furthest thing from science.

I was awful at science in high school and college. I took the least number of science classes required to graduate and no more, and I can't remember anything about the science I learned. I recognize that somehow, I've doubtless used it a little throughout my life without even realizing it. But when it comes to PTSD, for me, science is never part of the equation: I experience PTSD as a mental, emotional state that manifests in complex symptoms.

There is, however, something to be said for the science of PTSD. I just prefer to see PTSD more as the brain's reaction to traumatic experiences and what follows, rather than a science.

If you ask people, "What is the most important organ in the human body?" Most will answer, "The heart." You can't live without a beating heart. We place so much importance on it that we even attribute states of mind and emotions to our heart, including feelings and beliefs. If I'm emphasizing something I believe in, I will say, "I believe it with all of my heart."

In truth, we give the heart way too much credit. Emotions, our feelings, and our beliefs are not based on the heart…but on the brain.

It's All in Your Head … Literally!

The brain is the computer of our life. All that we do, feel, or think has to do with what's going on inside our heads. The brain directs every organ. It manages our movement. It manages the function required to work for us to live: breathing. And it's not until I understood the correlation between PTSD and its effects on the brain that many things in my life became clear.

A few areas of the brain are directly impacted by trauma and specifically have to do with PTSD. Unplug the brain, and everything else just exists. That's why the term "brain dead" indicates there's no chance of life without outside intervention. Turn a ventilator off, and if the brain is not sending the signal to continue breathing, that person dies.

The amygdala, prefrontal cortex, and hippocampus are the areas of the brain compromised during trauma, those areas continue to affect those with PTSD.

Areas of the brain are compromised during trauma and continue to affect those with PTSD.

The Amygdala

The amygdala of your brain sets off inner warnings or alarms to protect you. When I experience something disturbing or dangerous, the amygdala signals for me to feel fear. In actuality, it is the part of the brain that works to keep us safe. When it's in a normal state, that's exactly what it does. When it's in overdrive, it's hard to make sense of what is happening, so it confuses the brain into believing there is a threat that exists to us. And when the amygdala is confused, we tend to have an extreme response. It doesn't matter whether the response is real. The brain uses the amygdala to make sure we're safe.

Those who have PTSD frequently have extreme responses, even if whatever set off our reaction turns out to be a "false alarm." Perception is everything. If I perceive something as a threat, I will react to protect myself. We don't even do that consciously—it's subconscious. That way, we can keep the danger from harming us. So, our fears do not have to be based on fact. Even a normal reaction to something that scares us can be confusing. A loud noise that you hear suddenly, in a place where that noise is unexpected, can trigger the amygdala. It may turn out to be nothing, but when our brain has not yet put it all together, it confuses something normal with something abnormal.

The Prefrontal Cortex

Another area of the brain impacted by PTSD is the prefrontal cortex, which governs decision-making, how we portray our personality, and social behavior. It helps us put on the brakes when anything causes us to feel fear, until we realize that what happened or what's happening is actually not a threat. The prefrontal cortex works in concert with the amygdala to regulate our responses.

In people with PTSD, the prefrontal cortex doesn't adequately do its job when needed. PTSD causes the prefrontal cortex to be unreactive. It's like driving a car and pushing the accelerator to the floor—even when it's not needed—and then finding out the brakes don't work. That's why sufferers of PTSD feel anxious or have strong reactions to situations that have no reason to make us fearful. It can even cause us to avoid things that can trigger intense emotions and reactions and feelings.

The Hippocampus

Another area affected is the hippocampus, which regulates our memories. A traumatic event may cause the hippocampus to shrink and work improperly. And when that happens, we can't recall important memories when we need them. Worse, terrifying memories may pop up at the wrong time. This confuses our present state of mind.

Understanding how these parts of the—the prefrontal cortex, the amygdala, and the hippocampus—play a critical part in PTSD illuminates a lot. It can help us make some sense of the way we feel and act. It shows us why we often fail to think clearly enough to make good decisions or fail to remember important details, which can work negatively affect our feelings and reactions. In essence, the brain and the effect PTSD has on it directly influences our lives and those people who make up our support base.

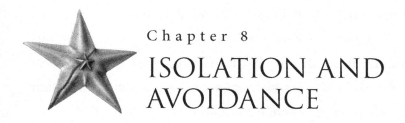

Chapter 8

ISOLATION AND
AVOIDANCE

All of my life, I never wanted to be alone. I didn't need "me" time. Recharging and relaxing alone was for other people—not for me. I am a chaplain. My work hinges on being around people, and that can mean long hours spent with others in need with very little time for personal rejuvenation. This worked for me for decades. Then PTSD happened and everything changed.

Isolation can mean so many different things to each and every person. During the era of Covid, people have been isolated or quarantined. Most have found isolation to be very trying. We are social beings, and even the most introverted among us need some interaction with others.

There are many layers to peel back on the issue of isolation related to PTSD. It's not black and white. It's not always about wanting to be alone or seeking a lack of stimulus. The isolation is also not only physical. I often feel isolation in my own thoughts, feelings, emotions, and actions. Any time I feel misunderstood, it brings about feelings of being utterly alone in this battle, feelings that so many will never understand. This leads to thoughts of shame and guilt, often exacerbating whatever symptom is most looming at the time. It can be so very lonely. And since we don't talk about PTSD like we do other issues, there is rarely ever anyone who truly understands how I am feeling. It seems whatever way I turn, there is just more loneliness.

The physical isolation, or the need to isolate, can come out of nowhere. On a totally normal day without much going on, I can find myself in such a state that I need to remove myself from any and all situations. This doesn't feel good. It feels like I have no control over my life from moment to moment. The physical isolation leads to emotional turmoil—*What is wrong with me? Why can't I just be normal?*—and before long, I am not only physically alone, but in a full-fledged shame spiral about my *need* to be alone. Why? Introverts who need or who enjoy time to themselves don't sit around beating themselves up about this part of their personality. So why do I? The spiral is never-ending.

I have at times forced myself to stay present even when red flags were going up all around me. This never ends well, either. By the time everything settles back down around me, I am an emotional bomb just waiting to explode. The slightest disturbance or conflict can send me completely over the edge. I can be cutting with my words and my tone in these situations. The people I love get hurt. More shame. More guilt. More thoughts of *I should know better.*

The other side of this coin is that others sometimes seek to isolate themselves from me. In my mind, I can understand why. When I am having a particularly bad day—perhaps I am feeling high anxiety, I am snippy, or I am quick to temper—this is difficult on people, especially the people I love the most dearly. At some point for them, it all just becomes too much. Too painful. They don't want us to hurt any longer, and they themselves do not want to be in pain.

This is human nature. Over time, people become worn down and tired after trying everything they know to do with no results. When nothing else works, they find more and more that removing themselves from me is the only solution. Everyone retreats to their places of safety and calm. Like I said, I understand why this happens. But understanding this dynamic and how it plays out doesn't make it any less sad and painful. There are so many negative emotions that bubble up from this: anger, guilt, shame, regret…it leaves me feeling like a failure.

> **Over time, people become worn down and tired after trying everything they know to do with no results. While understanding this dynamic is helpful, it does not make it any less sad and painful.**

I don't want to be isolated or distant from the ones I love. When I am physically separated from them, it hurts my heart, and I know it hurts them as well. I miss them terribly. I miss being able to just "be" with the people whom I love. I wish I could be symptom-free and fully enjoy the company of my family and friends. The emotional isolation it causes can even be worse than physically being apart. Being in different worlds while still being physically close is gut-wrenching, and I pray there will be a time in which I will overcome the need to isolate.

Isolation Has a Price

The tendency to isolate has not only impacted my personal life, but also left its indelible mark on my career: my ministry. There have been times that I could talk myself out of the tendency toward isolation. *Stop avoiding people, things, experiences, and actions when you now know you ought to reach out and be there and do the hard stuff.* I learned this by working as a chaplain at Walter Reed Army Medical Center. Every night one of us in the rotation performed the on call, onsite shift. I found it spooky walking around the deserted hallways of this ancient, creaking building. I wouldn't say I liked going to the psychiatric wards where I didn't know the patients to ask if I could speak to them about faith. I worried what the doctors and nurses would think of my feeble attempts at talking to these patients about faith. I worried about being rejected by very troubled, sometimes violent, patients. Once the "talking-myself-into-it" phase wore off, I started hiding out in the office, with indigestion, my stomach in knots, my breathing uneasy. I was miserable—controlled by my anxiety, self-doubt, and worry.

The head-chaplain had discovered from the staff that I hadn't been showing up to make my rounds on these wards. On one of those evenings, as I hid away in the office, he unexpectedly opened the door. He knew what was going on. He had read my anxiety and told me to get out of the office, face my fears, and make the rounds.

On this day, I was able to get up and do what was needed. But I can't say the same for every day. Living with PTSD involves a constant battle of the pull toward avoidance and isolation and pulling yourself up by your bootstraps and muscling your way through things that are simple for most people. I avoid conflict, I avoid situations that may make me feel frustrated, I avoid loud places, I avoid crowded places, I avoid certain movies, I avoid news related to war—especially terrorism—I avoid places that feel unsafe…I could go on and on. The avoidance makes me feel safe, but if I am being totally honest, I realize that this is a false sense of safety. My safety nets provide just enough "control" that I feel like I am winning. But with PTSD, sadly, no one is ever winning.

Isolation and avoidance wear heavily on my career, my ministry, my relationships, my mental health, and my faith. I hope people around me understand this has nothing to do with them and everything to do with me. If I could wave a magic wand and fix it all, I would.

When I'm in a room with other people, I tend to listen more than talk. That's totally outside my wishes and normal behavior. Now, though, it's become commonplace because of my PTSD. I know to others this can be seen as being antisocial, and that thought hurts. More than anything, I wish I could push past my feelings and be more social. The truth is, some days I simply can't. And on the rare occasions when I am able to push through, I find myself utterly exhausted afterward, having to completely isolate in order to recuperate.

I will keep fighting to "stay" even when everything inside of me is screaming to "go." I will keep trying. I will never stop.

Even if I grew wings and escaped, I would still be trapped by my own mind.

HealthyPlace.com

Chapter 9

FIGHT, FLIGHT, FREEZE, AND HYPERVIGILANCE

Growing up, my best friend and I did everything together, and we were optimistic about life. However, I always knew that if I asked my best friend's mother how she was doing, there was no way to get her to say anything positive. She'd never reply with something like "I'm doing good, thank you." Rather, it was a litany of woe-is-me talk. "I'm not feeling too well today," she'd say. Or, "I didn't sleep well last night." Sometimes, I'd try to avoid her altogether because of her constant negativity. At church, if I saw her, I would move over and go down a different aisle. It was my way of keeping us from coming face-to-face. In that way, I could avoid the negativity I knew would be awaiting me.

This is what happens with someone suffering from PTSD. Often, we feel the need to back off and get away from people. We need our space. There are times when we feel anxiety and know it. It's easier to retreat because we don't have to cope with what's happening and how that may affect us emotionally. If I can leave and go somewhere else, I will. It's my way of trying to deal with the situation. But I am well aware this is a far cry from "dealing" with a situation. It's simply a "flight" response.

If people describe how I was before PTSD, it would be very different from their description of how I am today. In the past, they would say something like, "There's nothing he won't go after. There's no argument that he can't make." In other words, I fell on my sword in every situation. I preemptively struck out to get a leg up in an argument. I was a master at not losing arguments. It rarely happened to me. I loved winning in discussions.

Yet after I began suffering the facts of PTSD, things began to change. I want to argue less and less now.

I always had an opinion because I wanted to be right. I've always said that everyone wants to be right. If you didn't want to be right, you wouldn't argue about anything. It wouldn't matter if you didn't want to win the argument. Some people take that to the nth degree. I must admit, I was really guilty of that until the last ten years, and I've experienced a slow regression from that desire.

Now, I avoid conflict whenever I can because when I encounter conflict, my anxiety level rises. Panicked, I try to figure a way to get out of it. With PTSD, because of the baggage and the emotional load we carry, some of us either choose fight or flight. We want to jump in and be right at no cost, or we want others to be wrong, so we argue with them to prove them wrong.

When I choose flight, I am always asking myself, *how can I get out of this? I don't need conflict right now.* And then I try to get out of it. One of the ways I avoid something is to just shut down. I try to walk away, and I don't answer or engage, especially if someone is still aggressively coming at me. Anyone who is aggressive toward me is a threat in my mind. They can be a real threat, but it doesn't matter whether it's real or not when you *perceive* something as a threat. Even if there is a chance that it's a threat, our bodies are trained to react as though there is a definite and imminent threat to our safety and well-being.

It doesn't matter whether a threat is real or not. When you perceive something as a threat, your body is trained to react as though there is a definite and imminent threat to your safety and well-being.

First comes the avoidance. I avoid situations and discussions and that takes me further into the depths. But isolating myself from people—on purpose or not—so many times…it's draining. They may even be attempting to understand me, but too often I perceive them as someone threatening to me.

When I see someone as a threat to my being anxiety-free, I take the road of least resistance. I get away. I shut down hearing what the other person says. When I can't go any further, I just stop continuing the conversation. When I don't have an answer and say I don't know, it's usually because I really don't know. That's one of the intimidating parts of PTSD. So many of my actions cause me to think things I really didn't want to do or think. At that point if I lash out, it's because I feel cornered. That's anger, and anger of course, is fuel for anxiety. The angrier I get, the more anxious I get. Then I tend to be more aggressive. In many conflicts fight or flight are the only two choices. You defend yourself by either becoming obstinate and standing your ground, or you emotionally move away and, hopefully, physically move away as well.

I believe that every honest church-attender must admit that, at least once, we wish we could listen to the Sunday sermon lying down. I had my prayers answered the day I was sitting in a worship service in Iraq, listening to Chaplain David Allen as he got to the meat of his message.

Suddenly, a boom could be heard in the distance. The loudspeaker blared, "Incoming! Incoming! Incoming!" That was the signal that we were experiencing a mortar or rocket attack.

We all dove to the floor. After a few moments of lying there, I thought, *We may be on the floor, but that's no reason to wait in silence.*

So, being the Baptist that I am, I yelled, "Preach on, brother!"

True to his calling, Chaplain Allen picked up where he had left off. While still lying there behind the pulpit, he expounded on the Word of God for at least ten minutes. It had to have been the best ten minutes of preaching I'd ever heard. Talk about having your cake and eating it too! After the all-clear signal, the whole congregation sat back down in their chairs and finished the service. It's incredible that even during an attack, we could continue to worship and hardly miss a beat.

The same can be said about spiritual warfare. Even in the worst of times, God will continue to bless and use us, if we surrender to His will. People continually asked how safe we were, and my best answer is, the safest place in the world is to be in the center of God's will.

In my many years of pastoral experience, I have witnessed many interesting events unfold in the middle of a worship service. Once, a wasp kept flying around my head as I preached. (I'm allergic to bee stings.) Another time, the electricity went off during an evening service. A drunk once burst through the sanctuary doors, thinking he was entering his house. Another time, my little daughter, Jennifer, pulled away from my wife, ran down the aisle, and clung to my leg while I attempted to preach. While none of these examples were the least bit humorous at the time, they were unforgettable.

That's not to say I don't have any humorous worship service memories. During my seminary years, I served as Minister of Music at Bridgedale Baptist Church in Metairie, Louisiana. The church was observing a baby dedication service, which was to include our fifteen-month-old son, Adam. Cherri and I stood in front of the congregation along with the other parents and children. Proudly, I held Adam in my arms. The pastor stopped in front of each couple, individually charging us with the responsibility to faithfully raise our child in the church. As he began his charge to Cherri and me, Adam stretched out his arm and with all his might, slapped me right in the face. I was mortified, but the congregation roared with laughter. Before long, the pastor completely lost it and joined everyone else. I remember it like it was yesterday.

All of this is to set the stage for what I experienced in Balad.

Our thoughts can be irrational, but that doesn't make them any less disturbing. I have always had a terrible fear of snakes. I realize that many are helpful and some others even kill venomous snakes. Somehow that doesn't really matter to me, because I'm afraid of any snake. Somebody once said the only good snake is a dead snake. I would like to offer that in my mind, even a dead snake is not a good snake. I'm not sure where my fear came from or why I've never overcome it, but it's bad—so bad that many times the fear of being bitten by a poisonous snake and dying from the bite has entered my mind, unprovoked. I relate to people who say that if a venomous snake bit them, they would more than likely die from shock way before the venom killed them.

Our thoughts can be irrational, but that doesn't make them any less disturbing.

I definitely have other fears in my life. Every other fear pales in comparison to snakes, though. I know it's somewhat irrational and to some people is probably completely irrational. That doesn't change the fact that it affects me the way it does. If someone were to put a rubber snake in a drawer that I opened, my reaction would not be based on seeing a fake snake. I could see myself screaming, running away as fast as I could, and possibly even knocking everyone down between myself and the door. The reaction had nothing to do with whether it was a threat or not. I would be responding to what I perceived to be a real threat.

Hypervigilance

Hypervigilance is an extreme state of alertness—being overly cautious. Our response results in behavior intended to prevent harm. Those who are hypervigilant are in a state of watchfulness. We observe and are much more aware of our surroundings than the average person. We are constantly—subconsciously—assessing our surroundings and how they make us feel. *Are we in any danger? Are we safe?*

Hypervigilance caused by PTSD is an ever-present state of extreme caution that undermines our life. The desire to protect ourselves causes us to become vigilant and to be watchful for real danger or a real threat that presents itself. It is the hypervigilance that allows us to act and react and keep ourselves from being harmed.

The problem of hypervigilance with PTSD is that it causes us to be watchful and more observant, to proceed with caution. All of which works to our benefit…when an actual threat exists.

When the threat is only presumed and not real, it can be damaging. Being on guard for many of our waking hours brings about extreme anxiety. It's easy to find hypervigilance coupled with situational awareness if we're often on alert, excessively scanning our environment. It has the effect of being completely emotionally draining.

Those with PTSD can relate to this troublesome feeling. It begins with the increased alertness. The heart begins to pound harder. It becomes difficult to concentrate because you're always checking out your surroundings. It's easier to get startled. So, we find ourselves in a place where we can easily be irritable. The mind usually enters a win/lose situation where there's no gray area. Everything is just bad or good, causing you to overreact to situations physically. Like an ever-present tingling sensation, causing the hairs on our hands and arms to stand up.

Fight, Flight, or Freeze

When I'm in an anxious situation or feel like there is a threat, I feel the need to react. Usually, without even recognizing it, I decide. If that decision is to handle the situation at that moment, it is known as "fight." It's an attempt to reduce the stress or neutralize the threat. At other times, I make the conscious decision to run (flight reaction).

Whenever I encounter a stressor, if I feel like I can handle it, I try to solve the problem. With PTSD, the threat is rarely a physical danger. More than likely, it requires an emotional reaction before deciding whether to handle the situation or separate myself from it. I will decide what course of action helps me the most in solving the problem—either fight or flight.

When I'm not able to decide whether fighting or fleeing is the best option, then freezing becomes my only other possibility. My body becomes paralyzed, and I just stare like a deer in the headlights. My response becomes a freeze reaction until my brain figures out a solution. So, ultimately, I either handle the situation or run away from it.

Our immediate response is subconscious. It doesn't require thinking about it. It's an in-the-moment decision shaped by experiences. In my case, PTSD drives my fight, flight, or freeze responses. I am merely a passenger, completely out of control—led by my subconscious and its wounds, controlling my thoughts, emotions, and reactions.

It's hard to say which reaction is best. It's often impossible to know which way brings about the best outcome. I react by instinct, based on experiences with similar situations. How vulnerable I feel and if I have the emotional energy to deal with it right then and there. I have a good idea of what's going to happen based on the decisions I make. Still, no matter what, there's no guarantee that I will make the right decisions.

We are oftentimes not in control of how our PTSD affects us and others, which is why vulnerability is a huge part of PTSD. It strips us of our control. It controls so many aspects in everyday life. Due to our vulnerability, and the fear involved in it, we feel like it threatens our sense of safety and security.

Part of the fear is if we relax into being completely ourselves—with all the flaws of PTSD—then it will just bring up feelings and emotions involving rejection, many of which we may not be ready to face. That's one of the drawbacks of talking to people about our PTSD. I feel like I have enough emotional pain, and it keeps me from feeling safe when I'm feeling vulnerable. It keeps me from opening myself up to other people about the truth of how PTSD affects me, as opening up to others would bring the possibility of their chastising or ridiculing me. Nobody wants that to happen. No matter who you are or what difficulties you're struggling with, being rejected only feeds into a fragile state.

Vulnerability

The sad fact exists that there has to be some willingness to be vulnerable to be healed in any way. Many times, that means learning to be vulnerable. We don't like to do things that are uncomfortable and cause us pain, so we shy away from them. All of this is part of our overall well-being—learning to be vulnerable with people who we trust.

There has to be some willingness to be vulnerable to be healed in any way.

To be vulnerable is to open ourselves up to possibly being hurt. It's hard for people to share personal parts of their life. Especially those parts that deal with the way we feel. But everybody who cares about you, wants to help you fix your issues. Period. Now I know that in general men have the desire to fix things. That's true in every area of our lives. The problem with that kind of thinking arises when we don't want someone else to fix *us*. That would mean losing more control because someone else is taking on the responsibility of making you better. But there's nothing wrong with that. It's important to be seen, to be heard, and to be understood.

Everybody has their opinions on what you should do and how you should do it in dealing with something like PTSD. These are merely opinions—not usually rooted in knowledge, or experience. Don't get me wrong, I love that people want to help me, but "help" is the operative word. Not fix me, cure me, or heal me. I want people to support me more than anything; to be by my side no matter what.

One thing we must remember is that PTSD often causes problems with intimacy, family relationships, and friendships. PTSD interferes with decision-making and problem-solving. Trust, intimacy, and communication all play a part. How people see us. The adage "hurt me once, shame on you, hurt me twice, shame on me" plays into the vulnerability; that if someone hurts us, trust erodes, whether they realize it or not. With families, our actions erodes the trust of those around us. Those closest to us. They're dealing with some of the same things we do, except from a different perspective. When our mindset is that the world is a dangerous place, trust becomes very difficult. Even in safe environments we can experience times when we are hypervigilant, on guard, and filled with fear of threats.

Merriam-Webster dictionary defines vulnerable as "capable of being physically or emotionally wounded" and "open to attack or damage, vulnerable to criticism." Dictionary.com adds "open to moral attack, criticism, temptation." To sum it up, vulnerability is opening ourselves up completely—no more masking or hiding. Brené Brown, a foremost authority on vulnerability, defines it as "uncertainty, risk and emotional exposure." Brown suggests that vulnerability is our most accurate measure of courage. To be vulnerable is to allow ourselves to be seen on an emotional scale. It's the core of emotions having to do with shame, grief, fear and disappointment.

While serving as a city police officer I responded to a very frightening call. The dispatcher received a call from a young child saying her mom's boyfriend was angry and beating her. Being in the area, I responded. When I turned onto the street, I could see a little girl crying on the side of the road. I stopped. She told me which house was hers. I pulled up into the front yard in my squad car. As soon as I stepped out of the vehicle, I realized the windows were open, and I could hear an argument from inside.

At that point, another officer arrived. I told him to go to the back of the house. I would go up onto the front porch and knock. As I ran up the steps, I heard a noise from inside. There was no doubt in my mind what that noise was: the sound of a shotgun shell being pumped into position to fire. With no thought or hesitation, fear grabbed me. I jumped off of the porch and ran to position myself on the other side of the car.

Will I get to safety before he fires a shot at me? I thought. In seven seconds, I got safely behind the squad car. Even today, though, I recall those few seconds as being a much longer period of time.

It was like the world went into slow motion. From the moment I jumped off the porch until I reached safety felt like an eternity. During that time, I realized I had made a critical error by turning away from the danger to run. Instead, I should have quickly backed away so I could continue to see what was happening.

For the first time, I understood the adage "my life passed before my eyes." I have never fully understood how quickly my brain raced through decision and execution in just seconds. It only took a split second to respond and jump into action and a few seconds to get to safety and draw my weapon. I expected to die right at any moment, but it never happened.

When the situation calmed down, the man walked out the door and surrendered himself with no weapon in his hand. I wondered if there had been a gun. It turned out that the woman would not press charges, so I could never go into the house and retrieve the shotgun. A little later, though, I gathered myself, walked back up to the porch, and looked in the window, noticing a shotgun propped against a wall. Though I couldn't verify it, there was no doubt he had pumped a shell into the chamber.

We can make several subconscious decisions in seconds while our mind figures out how to best handle the crisis. My reaction was to flee immediately. If I had stood my ground and fight, or if indecision caused me to freeze, I might very well not be here today.

That's how important the fight, flight, or freeze reaction is in protecting us. If our brain makes the wrong decision, we're forced to deal with the outcome. When I choose to fight, I face the danger of making matters worse. The flight reaction can be just as dangerous since I choose not to deal with the situation but avoid it. And I've found that not dealing with critical problems comes back to bite me later.

Though it's almost always entirely unconscious, some circumstance in the here-and-now can remind you of traumas suffered years ago. Never fully "discharged," the original fear or panic linked to that memory compels you to react to the current-day trigger as though what happened in the past is happening all over again.

Leon F. Seitzer, Ph.D.

Chapter 10

TRIGGERS

The word "trigger" implies something quick, volatile, and destructive, evocative of a weapon. With PTSD, triggers may be present events, circumstances, memories, flashbacks, etc. that have the power to bring us back to the feelings of our initial trauma. Triggers are an ever-present reminder that there are still tender places within us that need tending and healing.

While triggers are unique to each person, many PTSD sufferers struggle immensely with loud noises.

Anyone who has a pet, especially dogs, can relate to the impact of fireworks. July 4th and New Years are dreaded days for dog owners as they attempt to manage the high anxiety brought about by the booming sounds. Dogs will cower, whimper, whine, attempt to hide... they are absolutely miserable and distraught, and there is little we can do to help them. We just have to wait it out. It's painful for everyone.

Fireworks are a well-known trigger for veterans, too, as they often take the mind back to the sounds of warfare. Once triggered, it is difficult to reason with oneself that these are merely fireworks. To the person suffering with PTSD, they are *not* merely fireworks—they are explosions, gunfire—very real and present reminders of war. Traumatic feelings and emotions come rushing back out of our control. The loud, exploding sounds trigger the nervous system and fear and the need to protect set in. While others are enjoying the pops, flairs, and colors in the dark sky—looking up, cheering, oohing and ahhing—we are just bracing ourselves counting the moments until the sky is once again quiet and calm. Once the night is finally quiet, it can take hours to calm the nervous system.

Just like with pets, the fear, anxiety, nerves and high alert linger long after the "party" is over, leaving us physically and emotionally drained and dreading the next firework-filled holiday.

While fireworks are a common trigger for people with PTSD, it's actually not one that affects me. What does act as a trigger to me is when I hear the sound of a baby crying. That crying can stick with me. I really struggle; immediately, I start feeling anxious at the sounds of the cries. *What's wrong with the baby? Who is taking care of the baby?* It grates on my nerves. I know much of it has to do with the death of the four-year-old, but it's much more than my experience with her dying.

The baby crying really gets to me because we treated young Iraqi civilians. They would come to the base and be treated for war injuries, and they could even stay and be hospitalized if needed. When mothers would come in with a young child or infant, they would be confused and afraid. The sounds often involved crying out in pain. The mothers wouldn't leave their baby's side. Sometimes gentle coaxing was needed for the medical personnel to gain access and do their work.

During my many deployments, I had so much exposure to sorrow and crying. Strangely, it's only baby cries that really get to me. I feel compassion and empathy when I am with a crying adult, but I do not experience a visceral reaction like I do when I hear a baby cry. Every caring person in the world hates to hear a baby or young child crying in pain, but for me, it is a full-fledged trigger. Memories, flashbacks, anxiety, fear...it all comes bearing down.

Still, most people don't have the same reaction I described. Very few have a flashback memory and heightened anxiety. They don't need the length of time to calm down from that startled anxiety.

And here's where everybody's that way. We have so many different paths to go. When that happens, for the most part, it's only a passing thought. As soon as I thought about it, I stopped thinking, so I didn't sit there and get angrier. Sometimes it happens. How do you explain how different it is for other people? The pain is still the same.

Another consistent trigger of mine is a little unusual. It has to do with a car door slamming. When I'm in the car, and my wife starts to get out, I hurry to be first person out because when she opens the door, she has a tendency to slam it. The slamming car door is a sound that often triggers a reaction in me. Cars are so tightly sealed these days—slamming makes a physical impact.

In such a closed space, that slamming sound and quick change of pressure takes me back to the hundreds of times I hit the ground. The slamming resonates in my whole body, and I can immediately be transported back to war. People use the term "hit the deck" pretty casually these days, but that phrase was a reality for me and my fellow troops. We would be going about our daily routines, and all the sudden we would get the signal to "hit the deck." This literally means throwing your body onto the ground. It's not graceful. It's traumatic. You have very little time to think. Every time I hit the deck, I never knew if this would be the last time. I prepared to die each time. The cumulative effect of this trauma is immeasurable.

Until writing this book and examining my own triggers, I had never made the connection between the car door slamming and those hit-the-deck moments. As I think through it, it makes perfect sense now. To most, a slamming car door may be a mere annoyance. To me, it floods my body and mind with thoughts of terror, danger, and fear of death. It is very real. So real that I can't "talk" my body and mind out of their reactions. Believe me, I have tried.

So, I avoid the stimuli. I hurry out of the car before my wife. I change my behavior to avoid being triggered. It's just something I have "learned" to do to keep myself from spiraling.

I'm good at changing my behavior to feel safe. I have safety nets all around me these days. It doesn't feel great to live in such a web—it makes life feel really small. There's not much room for spontaneity or feeling carefree. I now live a very deliberate and measured life. It's a trade-off that makes me feel all sorts of emotions—anger, resentment, sadness—but it's just the way it is.

Recognize Your Triggers

When it comes to treating mental disability as a critical factor in improving, we must recognize our triggers. My triggers are different from the next person. Different things trigger a reaction in me, whether negatively or positively, than for someone else. When faced with danger, whether bodily or emotional, our brain does not react normally. Reactions are then controlled by the threat or danger that exists. Our senses become acute. With PTSD, trauma is not stored in the past—everything is very much in the present—just below the surface. The present loses to the fear, anxiety, and lack of control. The brain is stressed to the point where reactions are based on something that is probably not a real threat and is certainly not in the present.

Many of those who have PTSD explain it as going away or zoning out. This is certainly cause for concern. It means the brain can't process everything it needs to process. Imagine driving on the road and forgetting that you've passed where you want to go. You were "zoning." It's not that we don't realize what's going on. Our brain is always connected, tuned into where we are. It's just that our conscious side isn't relating to the surrounding events. Everybody's had that kind of experience. I will reiterate that those who have a disorder revolving around fear and depression are more likely to lose this connection from time to time.

When my wife is talking to me, sometimes I recognize what she's saying, but I'm focused on something else. Even though I hear, I don't listen. That frustrates and can even irritate the person who is trying to communicate with us. When my wife and I moved to the seminary campus, we lived in a trailer in the campus trailer park. Our trailer butted up against railroad tracks. Trains came through day and night, often clacking on the tracks, screeching with brakes, and surprising us with horns. We said we didn't know how we were going to live like this. It was literally ten feet from the back of our trailer to the tracks. Of course, our bedroom was in the back, at the end with the tracks. It was very difficult to try to sleep and have a restful night. Focusing on anything in the trailer could be difficult. I'd be trying to study, and my wife would be trying to read, or we'd be trying to watch something on TV. But over and over again, there was a noisy disturbance.

I wouldn't have believed it, but in time, my mind would begin to shut out some of the unwanted sounds. Before long, we got to the point where we could sleep better. The noise and disruptions continued, but our acute focus became less aware and compensated by our hearing it less and less. We finally reached the point where we could hear it but didn't continue to notice most of the time. Friends and family came to visit us from out of town, and when the first train would come through, they'd be shocked.

Inevitably, the first things that came out of their mouth were something like, "How in the world can you live here? I don't know how you get anything done. I could never live where you live." For them, the noise and disturbance were what the brain focused on.

The same is true of hearing and listening. Hearing is inevitable. When there is a noise, you hear it. Whether we pay attention or listen to it is a different story.

Some triggers are impossible to avoid. If our surroundings cause triggers, it is more difficult to alleviate. The ones we can do something with are generally based on relationships.

Something happens where our senses are totally overwhelmed by the sights, sounds, and feelings. We enter another place where we can consciously shut down. Only, the unconscious never shuts down. It keeps going to a place in the brain. We normally don't have access to those types of memories that come back as intrusive thoughts, flashbacks, nightmares, and PTSD triggers. It's important to note that these types of reminders can in many times overwhelm us with fear, anxiety, and unacceptable behavior. These things appear without warning.

Flashbacks

Flashbacks are nightmares experienced without being asleep. They are intense experiences of reliving the traumatic experience when we're fully awake. Flashbacks are so real. Flashbacks can come on suddenly and feel uncontrollable. If something startles me, it may not take me back to trauma, but it affects me more than it ever did before PTSD.

A curious thing about flashbacks is that you end up working twice as hard, asking yourself whether what you're seeing or hearing is actually

Flashbacks make it hard to live in the present because you are never certain if you can trust it or not. happening. Because what's real and what it seems to be are wholly interchangeable. When you're in a flashback, you don't realize it—not until it's over do you know, because there's a break. There's a unique form of clarity when you realize you're back in reality. Occasionally it makes it hard to live in the present because you're never certain if you can trust it or not. It's very tiring.

Do you know how I finally know when something is real? Because, in my wildest imagination, I couldn't come up with anything as detailed or vivid.

That experience can cause us to lose track of time and what's going on in the present. Flashbacks take us back to a traumatic memory. When the triggers occur in the form of flashbacks, everything about the trauma can immediately come back, to the point of hearing and feeling when it really was happening. The brain switches to past trauma. It's so real that even the senses come rushing back—what we saw, what sounds we heard, the sense of danger we felt.

At first glance, it can be difficult to imagine that these things come back so real. There are times when a memory comes back, even by smell. My father was a big Old Spice aftershave fan. There was something distinctive in that smell. And sometimes when I'm thinking of a particular event with him, I can really believe I smell the Old Spice. Having spent so much time as an EMT, there have been smells that were part of recovering bodies. There is an unmistakable smell that becomes etched in your brain when you recover a body that's been burned.

These intrusive thoughts are unwanted and come out of nowhere. They have nothing to do with what is happening or conversation at that moment. It's normal to have sporadic intrusive thoughts, but PTSD causes the thoughts to get "stuck" and they are hard to get rid of. They are persistent and cause me significant distress, due to their disturbing, unpleasant, and graphic nature...thus causing me to want to keep them a secret and not seek help because I feel ashamed.

It's like being stuck in a giant spider web. The harder I try to relieve myself of the thoughts, the more they entangle me. The more they increase in intensity.

Triggers and flashbacks can cause dissociation to those with PTSD. They may feel completely disconnected from themself and/or their surroundings.

Matthew Tull, Ph.D.

Chapter 11

EMOTIONAL
EXHAUSTION

A person with PTSD does not begin with an appropriate level of stress. I am always on heightened alert, even if there are no external stressors. The PTSD, and all its effects, is always there—underlying everything I do. Typical, everyday situations can feel like attacks to my system. Sometimes it's easier to feel attacked, because at least then I can rationalize the frustration and anger I am feeling.

I don't like this. I am not a confrontational person; it's against my nature. But like I have said before, PTSD takes and takes and then takes some more. It is a ruthless thief, stealing and distorting all that we are at our core. It has changed me. It has stolen parts of me that I fear I will never regain. It has wreaked havoc in my life. It has caused so much pain and suffering, not just for me, but for my whole family. When I think of all that PTSD has done, I do feel angry. I think anyone would. I don't want to be this way. I am so weary of it, weary to my bones. It's exhausting!

Emotional exhaustion is a significant symptom of PTSD. As I use my emotional resources attempting to cope with trying situations, my mental capacity becomes overwhelmed. I expend energy dealing with such things as conflict, demands on my time, and lack of support. So much is required that my capacity to care for myself and those around me is reduced. What often takes its place is defensiveness and conflict. All of a sudden, I begin to struggle. Only so much effort can be given to maintain the balance. This becomes a critical factor for PTSD sufferers who are already overwhelmed attempting to keep negative symptoms at bay.

The amount of energy it takes to hide the outward symptoms of PTSD is exhausting. We put on an emotional mask to conceal anything that would seem out of the ordinary. It becomes like a mental motor memory. After a while, we can get really good at concealing the struggle that's going on inside. In fact, it becomes an unconscious action, making it easier to keep our feelings from other people. While it is like second nature, that is not to say it is not totally exhausting in every way—physically, emotionally, and spiritually. Numerous things in life weigh heavily on us. Any time our minds are engaged in this battle to hide, mask, or conceal how we are really feeling, there is always a significant price to pay. Thus, I can easily become emotionally worn and burnt out.

The whole idea of a mask is to hide from someone or to hide something about ourselves. Another consideration is it's a way of controlling the situation. I've chosen to manipulate situations, so others never know what's going on or what I'm hiding.

We wear masks for many different reasons. Primarily, it's to protect ourselves from some pain, a shield against situations that might disturb us. We also put on masks as a way of hiding or not hurting someone else. Someone asks a question, and we mask our answer according to whether it will hurt or not. For example, say someone asks about their outfit, "How does this look?" It doesn't matter whether we really like it. Even if we can't stand it, that's not what we're going to say. Our desire is not to make the other person feel bad. So, we say, "It's good," "I like it," or even "It looks great." We don't answer truthfully to keep from hurting their feelings.

We don't just mask our words; we mask our actions, too. Numerous times in our lives, we will prefer not to do something, but we defer to the other person. Restaurants are one of the prime examples. My wife and I rarely decide what we're going to eat before we leave home. On a typical day out, we'll talk in the car, and it kind of goes like this:

"Where do you want to eat?"

"I don't know, where do you want to eat"?

Usually, the answer back from one or the other after that is "I don't care, anywhere you pick will be fine." But it's not always true. And there are several times when I said, "I don't care, you choose." Then, the choice she comes up with is not really to my liking, although that's not what I'm going to say. I'm going to say, "I'm good with that."

Interactions like this happen many, many times in our lives. If our brains wouldn't let us lie, then this world would be a very different place. Can you imagine answering truthfully to every question someone asked you? It would be a much better world in many ways, but it would also be a very uncomfortable world. I imagine we would avoid many conversations out of fear that we will say something we don't want to say since we're being held to the truth.

Much the same can be said for those who have PTSD. If we were open and honest about everything that we said, how we feel, and how it affects us, I'm afraid those around us would have a tough time understanding us.

When someone complains about the same thing over and over and over, day after day after day, we begin to turn it off. Either we don't ask a question that might lead to that answer or avoid them altogether. That's why avoidance, although not the best method of handling things, is the option we sometimes choose.

Like my best friend's mother, I attempt to avoid people who are always negative. If someone is regularly critical or complains, I tend to avoid or change the conversation. Being fully involved in a long meeting can also have the effect of making me feel numb and drained. Take, for instance, coming home after a long day and experiencing weariness. There is no physical pain or muscle fatigue because no physical labor took place. Still, we're worn out from the mental drain of a busy, tiring day. For those living with PTSD, normal, everyday occurrences seem to take a more considerable toll. I have always been a very deep feeler of my emotions, and PTSD has intensified this part of my personality. Tasks like engaging in meetings, running errands, and so much more leave me feeling like I have run a marathon emotionally. I feel completely drained. Even though pain in the physical sense is absent, the desire to relax still exists. I want nothing more than to sit down in my recliner and retreat—to emotionally unwind.

It takes a concerted effort to move forward when I am emotionally exhausted. Nevertheless, any resolution requires making an effort. We've all heard, "take it one step at a time," which is oftentimes good advice. What it doesn't take into account is the size of the step. Is it a baby step? A long or short stride? It also doesn't account for the speed of the step. Is it slow and careful shuffling? Are we taking the step at a normal pace? Jogging? Running? Do we take it with the aid of a walker or railing? Do we manage it with the assistance of another or on our own?

For me, one step at a time looks vastly different from how others would handle it, and vastly different from day to day. Some days I have enough in me to take a few easy strides forward. This accomplishment feels amazing. On other days, the steps are tiny—smaller than baby steps—which leaves me feeling like a failure. I can't ever seem to make long strides over an extended period of time.

PTSD is just too unpredictable. It is very much a daily battle. One step forward and two steps back...like a dance I don't want to be dancing...it takes so much effort just to do the simplest tasks. Frustration comes easily. *Why can't I?* thoughts start flooding my mind. Added to this already emotionally exhausting inner dialogue, people just do not understand how much effort I have to expend to

Those living with PTSD may need more sleep, more time to rest, more time unplugged from the world, more time alone to refuel for the next day ahead. just get through most days. Most people love a day filled with interaction. Others seem to have boundless energy. People do not understand that those living with PTSD need more sleep, more time to rest, more time unplugged from the world, more time alone to refuel for the next day ahead.

PTSD also makes me more emotionally invested. I have to be very careful about what I allow to enter my space. I have a hard time watching the news, intense movies or TV shows, or anything that heightens my already heightened emotional awareness. Topics or scenes will stick with me for days, while for others they may switch the TV off and never think twice about the images they saw. Not me. I find myself thinking and worrying long after processing information from the news. I find myself replaying intense scenes from movies or TV over and over in my mind.

There are daily memories of PTSD everywhere, its presence unceasing. Although I'm generally able to spend time during the day without feeling it so acutely, it's something that's hard to comprehend. I've never had as much empathy for a group of people like those suffering from PTSD. Most times it's like having a heavy weight on your back and taking it around wherever you go. It doesn't matter what you do—it follows you like a shadow. Most stressors bring it to the forefront. It engulfs my life throughout my days, months, and years. I don't think there's a time I can sleep without being affected in some way.

The emotion needed to keep it repressed so that others do not see PTSD in my daily life is exhausting. This may be anxiety at a time of fear or something that threatens to alter the balance. It's emotionally pushing down inside as my anxiety rises. If I'm sitting in a chair, my grip tightens, and my fingers dig into the fabric. Unfortunately, this is how I live my life. Pushing down is often a pressure that I put on myself. I want to lighten my load and possibly can do it, but as soon as I'm not alone again, I fail. Anxiety, tension inside almost never disappears.

I've discovered that I need to focus on something different than the tension. This change of direction could be my job, sitting in an office while working on a computer or writing something. In my work I deal with chaplains who have experienced trauma in so many ways…what many might call "unfortunate situations." In most people's lives, that's exactly what it is. You just find yourself in a place you don't want to be. But as soon as it's over, the effects fade. People simply resume a normal life. With PTSD the tension that presents itself is always just under the skin, waiting for something to trigger a sight, a sound, a smell, or other people.

The worse I become, the more I need to be alone. It's not a desired isolation. It's not as inevitable as it is necessary. One of the reasons for the isolation is the filtering of other situations and circumstances. When I go to my office or man cave, I'm all alone. I don't have the stress of carrying on a conversation. I don't need to be afraid about anything. I can pretty much control the situation. It takes a distraction, like being immersed in a movie or TV show, which allows me to shut everything else out and focus just on what's happening on the screen. Now, I have to admit that sometimes even this can cause tension if the distraction is related to triggers, or something related to traumatic events of the past. I equate it to ghosts from the past that haunt me continually. It's frustrating because those ghosts never leave me completely. And because they are in the past, I can't change anything. I am not in control. The past is set. It was a moment in time, only having existed then, but it continues to haunt me and drag me down.

It's hard to explain how depressing this constant emotional weight can be. When I work on a project that requires my attention for hours, or throughout the working day, I come home exhausted from emotional fatigue. That is caused by the amount of thinking and problem-solving it takes me to get through tasks. Many times, when I think about a task, I pick up my phone and set a reminder. With most of the reminders we can check off our list every day. Most of the time I can clear my plate. I don't need to repeat it every hour again and again.

But not so with PTSD. The anxiety tension involves anger, fighting, fleeing, isolation, and others. They can't just be checked off and forgotten. The problem is that an hour later I have to check off again, numerous times, day after day. So, when I say unrelenting, I mean that the effects just don't stop.

Those are the kinds of things many sufferers of PTSD juggle every day after day after day. That's why, when I come home from work, I am emotionally wasted. All I want to do is get into my easy chair and recline, sit back, close my eyes, and not engage.

The relaxing time I have in the evenings can still be interrupted. And if that happens, then the time that I can normally shut everything out by going to sleep at night is interrupted. It's hard to get to sleep. It's hard to *stay* asleep with my intrusive thoughts, dreams, and nightmares concerning negative thoughts and actions. Even the resting cycle of sleep is invaded. It's a heavy, weary long road...and every morning I wake up, it's still there.

People with PTSD and resulting fatigue have impaired judgment, reduced motivation, and increased risk for injury ... it makes it hard to do the things that bring you joy.

https://blackbearrehab.com/mental-
health/ptsd/ptsd-and-fatigue/

Chapter 12

MEDICATIONS

If you are familiar with *Star Trek: The Next Generation*, you know that the character Data is central to the series. Data isn't human but an android of sorts, driven by a positronic brain. Because he's a walking computer, he has the answers to all knowledge-based questions.

The one glaring difference between him and the rest of the crew is that he is unable to experience emotions. His creator built him without an emotion chip. He struggles with jokes because they're not grounded in logic. One of his most endearing characteristics is his desire to be more like the humans around him, his longing to experience emotion. He has no highs or lows, no happiness or sadness—no feelings at all. His response to any situation is a flat affect. In other words, he is a space-aged Pinocchio, a creature built by a man who wanted to be a boy.

In some ways, I'm like Data when it comes to emotion. As a person struggling with PTSD, my experience of emotions is different from that of many other people. One way of settling with that can be manifested through medication that help me navigate everyday life, designed to be taken continually. Many people living with PTSD takes at least one medication a day. Without medication, coping with even routine experiences can be difficult, if not impossible.

By design, psychotropic drugs prescribed for PTSD lessen anxiety, depression, and anger. However, while minimizing unwanted negative feelings and reactions, they also reduce positive aspects of one's personality. The medications shorten the breadth of the entire emotional spectrum. It is rare to feel extremely happy or sad. I can still feel highs and lows and sometimes react in the same way I used to in each situation. But often, the ends of my emotional spectrum are dulled or muted in no small degree. The same can be said for a vast majority of people with mental health disorders that are centered on emotion.

I still can't help but think that I am weak because my PTSD puts me in the category of more severe sufferers. Interestingly, my brain equates needing to take the drugs with weakness. I know better than to think that way, but that thought still exists to some extent. I'm thankful, at least, that ten years into my diagnosis, I don't feel nearly as much shame around taking medication as I did at the beginning of my treatment.

We can be anywhere on the broad spectrum of our emotions and personalities. If we're very sad, we can react by crying, talking to someone, or doing something that will pick us up. The medications take away the extreme ends of the spectrum. It's rare to feel extremely happy or sad. By design, psychotropic drugs level emotions so that the user experiences less anxiety, depression, and anger. The problem is that while minimizing the unwanted feelings and reactions, they also minimize some much-desired aspects of personality.

Psychotropic drugs level emotions so that the user experiences less anxiety, depression, and anger, but they also minimize some much-desired aspects of personality.

I see psychotropic drugs as Band-Aids, able to cover the wound and buffer the pain of contact, but without much healing power. They are what I have accepted to be necessary evils.

Living with PTSD is often about choosing between the lesser of two evils, between outcomes that fall short of ideal. In my struggles with PTSD, I have learned to navigate difficult forks in the road, with my choices ultimately leaving me feeling emptier than I would want. Rather than being able to achieve the satisfaction of overcoming, I live with the reality that I must settle for less in order to move forward. Moving forward is critical.

PTSD and Joy

What I miss the most is that the medications don't allow me to fully experience happiness. In the New Testament of the Bible, Paul said, "I can be content in whatever state I am in." I know that contentment doesn't wholly depend on how I feel or what I do, but has more to do with accepting who I am now.

We tend to see happiness and joy as one in the same. They're similar in the sense that one can follow the other—they can trigger each other—but they're different. I'm glad that if things are going well, I'm happy, which can lead to contentment, and sometimes I can even get to a place of pure joy. So, there's a correlation between the two, and they go hand in hand with the other. But happiness and joy are not the same.

The striking thing about how I experience PTSD is that I know how blessed I am. I've had some difficult experiences. Experiences where fantastic people have been around me. Men and women who have supported me over the years. They will always have a place in my heart. It's these people who make me happy. If I look back on my life, I can see that I have had so many more good things happen than bad things.

Most people who look at the scale of my life would say I have more blessings pegged out than disappointments and failures. Most would say I am blessed beyond measure. And perhaps that it just goes to reason that this should make me happy, and I'm guaranteed to experience joy. That is true…at least until I make the distinction between pre-PTSD and post-PTSD.

The problem is, before the PTSD, I would be joyful much of the time. Now, the positive end of my emotional spectrum is numbed. A part was utterly cut off, so I lost my joy. I can get excited and be happy about something, but it doesn't bring me the joy it once did. This hurts me deeply because I desperately want to feel those emotions. I'm indifferent to those feelings—because I simply couldn't access them after my PTSD diagnosis.

Many factors can play into numbing feelings. They could have something to do with the kind of thing that's happening to me at a certain point. The lost feelings themselves can and do take away the joy of life. I see happiness as influenced by circumstances and experiences. I see joy as being an overall state of being. Whereas happiness is an emotion, joy isn't. Feeling both is one of the things I miss most. If my emotions don't get down as much and up as much, then certain things are simply lost. That doesn't mean I can't find joy in bits and pieces according to those happy circumstances; the difficulty is that it's not a state of being, and that is a terrible loss.

It's one of those things that I sometimes ponder. There's a yearning to have that ecstatic part of my life back, so I can get excited about things again.

The last thing I want is to get to a place where my medications are out of balance again. In the past, I have experienced many negative consequences as a result of not having the right medications and doses. I'm just praying that I don't get short-tempered, ill, and snappy because of it. Only time will tell, but I'm really praying that I stay somewhat on an even keel.

**Choice of treatment (medications
and therapy) should be based on
the best scientific evidence, comfort
with the options, and consultation
with a physician, psychologist or
mental health professional.**

American Psychological Association,
Clinical Practice Guideline for the Treatment
of Post Traumatic Stress Disorder

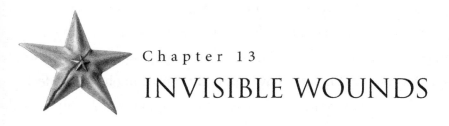

Chapter 13

INVISIBLE WOUNDS

I wouldn't wish PTSD on my worst enemy. It can happen to anyone, and it's mostly invisible—unless you know what to look for. The problem is it's not the same for everyone.

It's easier to spot physical injuries. People respond to those accordingly. Some people react to physical injury by keeping their distance from the afflicted because they're not sure what to say to them or do for them. Some react by acting like the injury isn't there. Others react by asking all kinds of questions. And it's not hard to see by people's reactions whether those reactions makes them feel uncomfortable or not. The same is true for people with PTSD: some want to be treated as normally as possible, while others are appreciative of the outpouring of concern and the expression of sadness that something like PTSD could ever happen to someone.

One thing is for sure. When someone who is injured interacts with someone they encounter, it can result in an uncomfortable conversation. If it's hard to relate to and interact with a person injured by trauma, then think about just how hard it is when others cannot see or judge the extent of your injuries because they are not visible. Those who suffer from PTSD often have difficulty explaining how they feel to a person who has no point of reference for the emotional injury.

Many discussions about PTSD revolve around why so many troops coming out of the Gulf War suffer from PTSD. We've never had this many veterans suffering from PTSD in the past. Part of this answer lies in the advent of Kevlar in our body armor and helmet, plus the "up-armoring" of vehicles.

Over the past twenty years, military vehicles have been modified and updated with additional armor. In past wars, many of those who were in close proximity to explosions died. In the Gulf wars, the added protection has resulted in fewer deaths in explosions. Many more of our troops survive the blasts and return home, wounded, but alive. Most who were exposed to the worst fighting now live with the horrors of the trauma and this debilitating disorder.

In years past PTSD was referred to it as "shell shock," and "battle fatigue."Mainly due to soldiers being exposed to artillery fire at close range. The loud and startling firing of those weapons, along with the percussion, shook soldiers. In 1980, the American Psychiatric Association began using the term Post-Traumatic Stress Disorder.

The battle we wage is on the inside—unseen.

It's almost impossible for someone else to understand the intense pain associated with PTSD when they've never felt it themselves.

People are often asked to describe physical pain on a scale of 1 to 10. One being no pain and 10 being the worst pain you've ever experienced. Because we've all felt physical pain, we can get an idea of how severe the pain is by the number someone chooses. We even get an idea of the type of pain they're feeling. Before I had PTSD, I didn't understand the emotional pain, anxiety, and fear those living with disorders were feeling on a constant and continual basis.

Family and close friends of those with PTSD often go through this progression of feelings: at first, they hate PTSD but love the afflicted. Over a period of having to deal with the negatives of PTSD, they merely care about the afflicted. Later, they get tired of how the PTSD has affected their life, and they begin to resent the afflicted. In the end, they can come to hate the afflicted. The passage from love to hate happens in phases. It's what I refer to as "The Attachment Slide."

The "Attachment Slide"

Love ⟶ Care About

Care About ⟶ Resent

Resent ⟶ Hate

Shame and PTSD

Shame is of the many unwanted emotions that holds back those who suffer from PTSD from sharing and healing. Shame is when you have negative feelings and thoughts about mistakes you've made or inadequacies you perceive within yourself. If we shame ourselves enough, it can severely affect our outlook on life and disposition while also influencing our performance. Likewise, we may allow others to shame us, too.

When I put myself down in thought or speech, I know what I'm feeling. I base my thoughts on those feelings. The part that doesn't yet exist is the hurt. What I usually think doesn't affect the emotion or feeling. If someone shames me, I don't know their intent. It's their actions that make the shaming hurt us so deeply.

We all like to think that we usually have the best of intentions, misguided or not. We attempt to reconcile our thoughts with our image. When I think of an image, the first thing that comes to mind is a photo. It's a moment in time, captured either by a picture or video. But not so with our images of ourselves. My feeling is that while my appearance or voice have not changed, I'm not as good of a person as I was before. I feel I'm not the man I used to be. I disappoint people more often now. My numbed emotions constitute a significant limitation. I'm not as talkative and engaging, which has resulted in limitations within relationships.

I find that I'm ashamed of my PTSD.

- *Ashamed* of having my adverse and irrational reactions due to PTSD. My responses don't often match the stimuli—because I am always "glass half full" of whatever symptom is dominating the day.

- *Ashamed* that I'm not able to put it into words, so that other people understand, or at least know what I'm thinking.

- *Ashamed* that I can't be who I once was.

- *Ashamed* that I can't adapt to who I am and who I say I am.

- *Ashamed* that I can't beat it—even though beating it should not be the goal. If we set goals too high and don't attain them, we have the tendency to give up. (That's why I tell people to set realistic goals. Realistic is a good word for describing what I want.)

- Simply *ashamed* because of survivor's guilt.

My mind isn't as straightforward as it was before PTSD. These days I can't seem to get everything together. I have to think a little longer before answering a question. My life is out of sync.

Out of sync is a good description of life with PTSD. When I'm watching TV and the speaker's voice is out of sync with the movement of their lips on the screen, it's extremely irritating and unnerving. All I can think about is the voices being out of sync. The story itself grows unimportant. I get lost in the problem instead of paying attention to the message. Being out of sync takes over and becomes the focus, the driving force.

I want so much to be normal again. But constantly being out of sync—constantly feeling this imbalance—keeps me from getting "normal" right.

Studies have consistently found a strong association between shame and the experience of PTSD symptoms following a traumatic event.

American Psychological Association
Differential Relationships of Guilt
and Shame on Posttraumatic Stress
Disorder Among Veterans

Chapter 14

MEMORY

My mind tries to protect me from things that will cause me pain. Very often I'll find myself thinking about memories that have been dormant or forgotten. When faced with a threat, I quickly turn away to protect my face.

These actions are split-second decisions. They're not something I think about at all. I just react. My subconscious senses danger, and I do whatever possible to mitigate it. The question that comes to mind when I think about a memory like this is a question of reality. If my brain can block memories as traumatic as this, then how many others are isolated? No matter how hard I try, I don't remember.

It is disconcerting to know that when I least expect it, a hidden memory may pop up because of some trigger. It's yet another example of my not always being in control. I realize my brain is deciding what or what not to remember. But just because a memory isn't remembered, doesn't mean that it doesn't affect my life. I don't know how many traumatic events I've been a part of but can't recall them.

Most of us have worked on a jigsaw puzzle at some point in our life, only to discover there are one or more pieces missing. We think those little bits and pieces don't make much difference, and most of them don't. Overall, they definitely *can* make a difference. How many of us would display a puzzle with missing pieces left out? No matter how many pieces there are that form a beautiful picture, when people see it, they will immediately focus on the one or two that are missing.

Often, when my lack of memory bothers someone, I feel apologetic. I'm constantly having to say sorry for not remembering something. I find it belittling and impossible to defend.

Memories save some of the best times in our lives; some moments are so wonderful that we'll never forget them, and they bring us positive feelings and happiness. I am just remembering to keep as much of the good as I can. Contrary to these great memories involving positive emotions are the things we would rather not remember, things that happened to us that may have crushed us at points at different times in life. Events like when 9/11 unfolded before our very eyes. A loss of a family member or friends. There are a plethora of things in my life that I try not to think about.

One of the most frustrating things about memory is that there are too many things I want to remember but can't. Sometimes that causes me sadness, depression, or frustration. This happens with many PTSD sufferers—there are details they wish they could remember but cannot. For example, someone in an auto accident may have no memory of what happened. Shock is one of the factors there, but I believe many times it's our brains controlling what we're allowed to remember for protection, and thus extremely traumatic moments can get repressed.

Deployed to Haiti

During the 1990s, Haiti went through some devastating times to prop up the government. The UN sent in troops, and the U.S. was part of that. I was tapped to deploy to Haiti. In many ways, it was supposed to be a humanitarian effort. During that time, most of my job was to collect items sent to me from throughout the United States, such as baby formula, clothes for all ages, school supplies, diapers, and toiletries. My chaplain assistant and I spent much of our time traveling to hospitals, orphanages, schools, and medical facilities to distribute what had been sent. I'll never forget many of the sights and sounds: people were so poor that they were living on the streets, and criminal activity was extremely high. When you're starving, especially if your family is starving, you have no way to provide for them, so you'll do anything to feed them. It was an incredible time where I got the chance to care for people.

On the first day, we flew into Port au Prince and disembarked from the aircraft. I was met by a military member whom I was replacing. After a few moments of niceties and welcome, we piled our belongings and ourselves into his vehicle to travel to our makeshift base. He immediately announced that a ferry had sunk a few miles off the coast in Port au Prince. The water was deep there. A squall had popped up and turned into rough waves. There were four hundred souls on the ferry. Panic ensued, and too many moved to the same side of the ferry, which in that weather offset the balance. It capsized and sank. All the passengers who could not escape before it quickly sank had died that day. We had arrived, hours after it happened. I was trained in critical incident debriefing, and the next morning, we went to the capital and taught it to high officials within the government.

As the recovery of bodies began, a horrific thing happened. Divers had to go down and recover the bodies that had been there for over twenty-four hours by that time, after which point the body expands. So, our divers would go down, pull bodies out, and let them go. The bodies would shoot up to the surface of the water. Those of us who were in medium-size boats would recover the bodies.

That image doesn't go away, ever.

Bodies were pulled out from the wreckage, deep down in the water. When a body came to the water's surface, it came with such force that it would pop up, like a dolphin jumping to the surface. Multiple bodies were being freed and emerging from the water this way. Every negative emotion that could be released at the moment, was—and, worse, the senses of touch and smell added to the horror. Just like that of a burning body, body, a person who drowns and stays under the water begins to decompose. When we grabbed the bodies from the water and sat them down into the boat, their skin would come off onto your hands. It would stick to you. Everything about this accident was already horrific, but this took it over the edge. But when you literally pick up a body, set it down, and the skin comes off...it is devastating.

Talk about being traumatized. These eighteen and nineteen-year-old soldiers would probably be scarred in some ways for life. That kind of thing is impossible to forget. But it can also be removed from our memories, stored in a place that protects us from living that nightmare. I'm not sure when it happened, but years ago, my brain shelved those events. It is wrapped up in a cocoon inside the brain. I never talked about it or thought it through for the last fifteen or twenty years. Then, last month, my wife was on the phone with someone, not knowing that I was within earshot, and something she was saying drove me to not only hear them in the background but start listening very closely. Whomever the person was, my wife was telling them about this horrific event that I had experienced. She described how difficult it was for me. Immediately, images flashed back in my head.

The Past Becomes the Present

I almost lost my balance and caught myself with the kitchen island. There was no gradual rise of anxiety or shaking. Instantly, it saturated my body and my emotions. I couldn't believe that it was so vivid in a split second, after all this time of pushing it out of my memory. The threat of PTSD grabbed me with such force that I had my jaws clenched hard enough to cause me discomfort. I began to process what had just happened. I had questions to which there were no answers. It happened. It was years in the past. And yet, it was like the past was the present. I isolated myself upstairs in my office, away from anybody in the world. *How could I be punched that hard, after so long, and with no conscious reminders of what had transpired?*

Something happens where our senses are overwhelmed by the sights, sounds, and feelings. It's another place where we can consciously shut down. Only, the unconscious never shuts down. It keeps going to a place in the brain. We usually don't have access to those types of memories that come back as intrusive thoughts, flashbacks, nightmares, and PTSD triggers. It's important to note those types of reminders can easily overwhelm us with fear, anxiety, and unacceptable behavior. These things appear without warning.

Flashbacks are so real. They can cause us to lose track of time and what's going on in the present. They can take us back to traumatic memories. When the triggers occur in the form of flashbacks, everything about the trauma can immediately come back to the point where even the senses of that moment in time come rushing back— what you saw, what you heard, the sense of danger you felt.

My father was a big Old Spice After Shave fan. There was something distinctive in that smell. And sometimes, when I'm thinking of a particular event with him, I believe I can actually smell the Old Spice. Similarly, having spent so much time as an EMT, there have been smells that were part of my recovering bodies. An unmistakable smell becomes etched in your brain when you recover a body.

I've recalled startling memories in my life. Still, none compared to my continued shock at being able to set it aside with no idea it's even there. I accept there are memories I have unwittingly shelved somewhere within my mind. Not having answers but having plenty of questions adds to the mystery surrounding my understanding of my PTSD.

Chapter 15

MENTAL HEALTH

I t is extremely important to understand the relationship between PTSD and mental health. I could not have progressed to the point where I am today if not for the psychological and emotional support of behavioral health professionals. Some of the most complicated work I've had to endure is the therapeutic relationships I have developed.

While I know some people will never seek this type of help, it is important to note that I believe there is no healing without others. Considering the stigma that is attached to seeking mental health treatment, I'm not at all surprised by the reluctance of some people to seek out treatment.

One of the reasons that chaplains are in so much demand is the privileged communication that exists between them and their counselees. Sufferers of psychological disorders usually desire the help they seek to be private and receiving help can easily be misconstrued as a weakness that needs to be hidden.

I believe the idea of giving myself permission to have PTSD is multifaceted. It's a complex work that is still in progress. For the most part, I did get to a point where I said it's okay for me to live with PTSD and know that I do have it.

One of the hard parts of PTSD is the embarrassment it brings. It's **One of the hard parts of PTSD is the embarrassment it brings.** embarrassing to me because I still can't reconcile my reasons for having PTSD. I think of just what that means to other people. Will they question whether I deserve to be diagnosed with PTSD?

We usually use "deserve" in a statement referring to good things, wondering if we have done enough, said enough, experienced enough to qualify? I know I still have a problem with that today. If I were counseling someone else dealing with the stigma, I would tell them they should have absolutely nothing to be ashamed of. That goes back to the stereotype of either being weak because I couldn't handle what had happened or having a lack of faith.

Mental health disorders are very real in the lives of many chaplains. While some have sought help for these disorders and received it, others still cling to the notion that they can't have them. During my treatment, the psychiatrist told me numerous times that my biggest hurdle was not giving myself permission to have PTSD. My logic was based on believing I didn't deserve to be in that category. My condition didn't begin to improve until I gave myself permission and accepted that PTSD wasn't a weakness. My prayer is that many others suffering the effects of PTSD will give themselves permission, too.

For military members who deployed to war, there is a sudden transition. One day you're in a war zone, experiencing fear, danger, and threats. You never feel safe. You're hypervigilant. Then, in the next twenty-four to forty-eight hours, you're transported back home. We use the term shock in distressing situations, but the few days after they return is one of the most shocking periods of time a soldier can experience. It's a full 180-degree shift in their environment and settings.

In the whole scheme of things, almost everything is inconsequential compared to life in a war zone. So much of what happens at home becomes small stuff to us when we return. I don't mean to downplay how important decisions are back home. What I prioritize as "big" is formed by my experiences.

What happened to me—and to a lot of other people—was that when I came back home, I couldn't make simple decisions. It didn't matter where we were going to eat. I was alive. I'd eat wherever anybody wanted to go. Do I want to see a movie? Did I want to engage in any activity? I thought, *I'm here. I'm with you guys. You decide.* I thought I had no problem because nothing measured up to the life-or-death decisions I'd had to make while I was deployed.

Our thoughts can be irrational, but that doesn't make them any less disturbing. Reactions to irrational fears has nothing to do with whether it is a threat or not. I respond to what I *perceive* to be a threat.

Proximity to tragedy is everything. Not just in the sense of location, but also emotionally. For instance, when we see tragic events unfold elsewhere in the world, we might very well be moved to the point of making a monetary donation to help. If we hear about a child missing anywhere in the U.S., we may feel sympathy for the family and pay more attention to the news reports. If our own child were missing, our world would be turned upside-down. Finding the child would become the focus of our existence. The very thought of such a thing stirs feelings of anxiety in me as I write these words.

Television has afforded us an instantaneous view of tragic events taking place around the globe. How many of us can honestly say we've never been touched by images of starving children in third-world countries, images so powerful that millions of people have already committed to supporting their plight in some way? Some find satisfaction in donating to world hunger organizations, while others sponsor individual children through trusted charities.

Being close to someone who has PTSD brings the pain, emotional distress, and behavioral upheaval into close proximity. It means the amount of time and emotional investment required is all too real. The more we care about them, the more it affects us as we interact. Some might say it rubs off on us. The closer we are to the symptoms, the more we feel it.

Mental Health Notes

In an effort to help others better understand the mental health side of PTSD, I'm including the following psychiatric session notes. These notes are completely unedited and are in the words of the psychiatrists' and psychologists' actual accounts of sessions with me. These notes are by no means accounts of all sessions but will hopefully provide the reader an honest insight into the therapeutic process.

***Patient reported his overall mood was "good." Patient reported no changes in his irritability and difficulty with making minor decisions. He noted that he continues to have problems "staying asleep" and frequently wakes up during the night. He noted that wanting an improvement in the quality of his sleep is a prime concern.

He reported that he continues to have trouble sleeping and described disturbed sleep every night over the past week. Patient said he might be dreaming but cannot recall the content. Patient reported ongoing symptoms of irritability, which are most likely to emerge at home with his wife. Patient said his wife and daughter continue to report that the patient is emotionally distant. Later in the session, the patient acknowledged that he felt "anxious" today, and during the session, which included "tightness in his chest."

He said that since beginning therapy, he has had to think more about past events that he has tried to avoid, which has invoked increased anxiety and symptoms. He expressed extreme difficulties in three areas: having physical reactions, trouble remembering parts of the stressful experience and trouble sleeping. He also described problems of disturbing memories, avoiding reminders, feeling irritable, and difficulty concentrating.

During the session, patient expressed several possible stuck points, including thinking he "should" not have a problem because there is no logical explanation for it, "fear of death is selfish" (which relates to religious beliefs), "the most important thing is taking care of other people," "I don't want my problem to affect me in an adverse way," "other people do not understand what I went through" (including wife and daughter can "sympathize with me, but not empathize with me"), and "I am to blame" (for the way patient's PTSD is affecting his family).

****Patient used his A-B-C worksheet to process two feelings since the last session. One feeling ("upset") involved the belief "I should not be experiencing anxiety." We explored this, and the patient acknowledged that not feeling comfortable validating his emotions was an ongoing stuck point. Patient's belief that "my experience was not as bad as theirs" underpins this stuck point. Patient also revealed, "I should be held to a higher standard" because he is a "man of the cloth." Patient added, "I should do better than most people because I set an example." Patient noted that he has "great faith that I have God in control" and said that this belief should alleviate his concerns. Patient reported that he has made some progress in accepting that he has "symptoms," although he still gets stuck on "why" he has symptoms. Patient said, "I still have problems with that, but I just accept the fact I do."*

***Patient described a dream he had about a week ago. In the dream, patient presided over a funeral service for a service member (something he said he does frequently) and presented the folded flag to the widow, who refused it and asked that it be given to the deceased soldier's parents. The patient tried to give the flag to the parents, who also refused, saying it should go to the wife. The patient attempted again to give it to the wife, who said, "I don't want you to give it to us. Give it to someone else. It's your fault he's dead." Upon waking from this dream, the patient said he was "upset and sweating" and noticed he was "hot and wet" before. Patient said he was "frustrated" over the dream since he "didn't understand why he was having this dream at all," adding, "I know exactly what you do at a funeral. I've done it before."

Patient's dream reflects the many levels in which he struggles with his emotions relating to his traumatic experiences. It demonstrates the significant self-worth the patient derives from being a chaplain and the anxiety invoked by the fear that his increased PTSD symptoms may make him less effective in giving effective care to others. It also speaks to the degree to which the patient attempts to deny his worthiness to have PTSD and the anxiety provoked by feeling he is not as worthy as others who may have sacrificed more.

That the soldier's death could be the patient's fault is symbolic of the patient's struggle with balancing his belief that the military (for which he is a symbol in the dream) is a force for good with the reality that bad outcomes can befall from military actions.

———————

***Post-traumatic stress disorder: Patient, without a biological predisposition for psychiatric disorders, without exposure to traumatic events in childhood, with exposure to trauma during work as EMT, with vicarious exposure to trauma as a chaplain, with supportive family presents with anxiety symptoms consistent with PTSD following numerous exposures to indirect combat and human suffering during deployment to Iraq.

Patient was advised that vicarious exposure to trauma can lead to PTSD. Patient and I discussed his ambivalence about receiving the PTSD diagnosis, given his role as a healer/caregiver. During this deployment, he was exposed to indirect combat, numerous medical casualties in the Balad Air Base ER, and vicarious exposures to trauma through pastoral counseling. The patient indicates that his wife and family noticed changes in his behavior after returning home, which led them to encourage his referral to Behavioral Health. Patient admits that he was resistant to acknowledging such changes given his role as healer/caregiver/chaplain. His exposure felt minimal and insignificant compared with those of other service members.

***Patient reports that since 2008 he has experienced daily anxiety, restlessness, muscular tension, and intrusive memories of trauma. Amnesia for some aspects of the traumatic events, irritability, middle insomnia, anhedonia/social isolation, emotional isolation from family members, avoidance of movies/tv-shows that remind

him of Operation Iraqi Freedom war increased tearfulness and emotional fragility. Patient denies dysphoria, fatigue, anorexia, feelings of guilt/worthlessness/hopelessness, suicidal ideation, flashbacks, and nightmares. Patient notes that he has never sought psychiatric/behavioral health help before but recognizes that he needs help to address ongoing anxiety symptoms that haven't responded to family and peer support and prayer.

Psychiatric history. Patient denies childhood exposure to trauma but was exposed to medical trauma while working as EMT. He reports vicarious trauma exposure via pastoral counseling as a Chaplain. Patient denies previous Behavioral Health treatment, including the use of psychotropics. Patient denies past or present Suicidal Ideations, self-harm, intent or plan to harm self, violence to others. Patient denies psychiatric symptoms prior to 2008 and denies hypomanic/manic symptoms. Not psychologically abused.

Patient said he continues to experience hyper-arousal (as "anxiety") and some degree of avoidance (such as not wanting his back toward people). Patient added that his wife has observed he now backs his car into parking spaces, which he did not do before. Patient noted an increase in symptoms over the last week due to thinking about and writing his Trauma Account.

***Patient did not appear to express feelings about the event as he read his account, despite the fact he recalled crying when holding a dying baby in his arms. Patient also reported a similar experience when

he read this account to his wife ("I didn't feel emotional"). With prompting, the patient continued to have trouble acknowledging emotions experienced and continued to have gaps in what he remembered. Of the baby, the patient said, "I don't remember her being alive? They say she died in my arms. I remember holding her and crying? I prayed for her family." Patient also had unanswered questions about the event: "Why did I hold her? I don't pick up and hold patients." With prompting, the patient revealed thoughts about the event, including "You could not imagine someone doing something like this to someone like that" and "Not only was she dead; it was so senseless." When asked about feelings of anger over the event, the patient said he experienced "more pain than anger," adding, "I don't recall as much the anger." Patient was more comfortable speaking about the positive aspects of that day, mentioning "how proud" he was of the actions of the chapel staff that day and also how he experienced the "highest highs" as well as the "lowest lows." Patient reported that the discussion about "vicarious trauma" had "resonated with me," and he has been thinking about how all his past experiences helping others have contributed to his present level of stress. Patient remarked, "I really carry what people tell me."

***Patient explored how he has improved his thinking around the stuck point "I don't have the right to have PTSD" and continues to struggle with "I shouldn't have PTSD." Patient noted that feelings of "embarrassment" and thoughts of "weakness" continue to

complicate the latter stuck point. Patient explored how his desire to please others and not disappoint others complicates things.

———————

***Patient reported frequently speaking with another chaplain who is also receiving care at DEFENSE STRESS MANAGEMENT for PTSD, although, patient described attending to his friend's needs rather than sharing experiences.

Patient remarked, "It's emotional for both of us, although he's having a harder time than me." Patient added the discussions "cause me to think of my past," although he is not likely to discuss them if he perceives his colleague as more in need.

Patient's ongoing worry for others and minimization of his own concerns suggest General Anxiety Disorder is a likely secondary diagnosis given that the patient's dysphoria appears secondary to his worry. Patient's desire for order and control also suggests OCPD traits. These conditions, along with associated safety risks, will continue to be evaluated.

———————

***The patient indicates that he is satisfied with his current functioning; however, he continues to complain about forgetfulness. We discuss the impact of anxiety/PTSD on memory and concentration and agree to monitor for the next several months. He denies a negative impact on work functioning or safety. Patient reports that he's observed an increase in "forgotten memories"

about other past traumas: ""ve thought about things that I had long since forgotten...I have remembered how frightened I felt at those times." We discussed how the patient also had amnesia for his OIF incident that brought him to Defense Stress Management for help, and perhaps how these memories no longer need to be guarded against as his anxiety improves. He has more effective tools to cope with emotional trauma. Patient and I discussed the mental defense of repression and how it appears to play a prominent role in his mind's defensive structure.

Patient's emerging memories of past trauma throughout treatment — combined with his complaints of amnesia for the OIF trauma — strongly suggests repression as a key psychodynamic defense. As the threat of the patient's memories and the availability of intrapsychic coping mechanisms grows, the patient's repression is less necessary, and memories begin to emerge.

***Patient and I developed an exposure/behavioral strategy to target his hypervigilance during dinners in restaurants. Patient and I reviewed conditioning theories as a model for the development and maintenance of anxiety/PTSD. The patient agrees to sit with back to other diners for 10 minutes during each meal for three dinners, and then move to the preferred seat for the rest of the meal (i.e., facing other diners). The patient agrees to extend the time spent facing away from other diners in subsequent meals until he can sit for an entire meal facing away. Patient and I will review his progress in future sessions.

***Patient reported an increase in dreams that involve "someone being injured, hurt," although the setting for the dreams is not always places from past deployments. Patient also reported, "I'm back to withdrawing some" and described withdrawing from his family when home in order to be alone in his bedroom. Patient also described "not liking to be around crowds," which he described as a new concern that he had not experienced in the past. Patient described an increase in "shakiness," and found the shakiness can arise anywhere, including being out with family and in the office.*

***(Wife) Collateral interview with patient's wife. Patient's wife reported two primary concerns in the patient: 1) ongoing tremors ("hands shake quite a bit"), and 2) minimizing emotional pain ("way blasé" and "I can't care attitude"). The wife reported that the patient may be avoiding discussing his concerns due to her health issues (being tested for cancer) and her need to care for her ailing father (who lives in their home). The wife also reported that the patient has increased occupational stress due to his promotion. The wife stated she is concerned about the patient taking medication due to the tremors and her belief that he continues to experience unresolved issues secondary to PTSD. The wife observed that the patient appeared "more irritable" on the days he had these sessions. The wife asked how to address avoidance with her husband. Literature was provided on the relaxation skills-building phase of*

EMDR and how patients are encouraged to share these activities with spouses. The wife was also given tips on how to engage with the patient in 1-1 activities as a means to create a relaxed space for the patient to share or for the wife to ask questions. The wife expressed thanks for the phone interview, and the ongoing treatment the patient is receiving.

***Patient described "rising anxiety at times for no reason" and "thinking about a lot more things these days." Patient noted that some of the things he is thinking about (e.g., his wife's health, work issues) are "sometimes sad," which "raises anxiety." Patient also described recalling new memories from new deployment ("something now has come up that's flooding my memory"), including remembering an incident in which an 18-month-old baby had 3rd degree burns over 80% of its body. Patient recounted how difficult caring for this baby was for the staff, given that they were not accustomed to working with burn patients, saying, "the staff took a beating seeing the baby in pain." Patient imagined that the baby died after being stabilized and discharged since this was not uncommon once locals were sent to Iraqi hospitals. Patient remarked, "I wish I had a way to know what happened to these folks? I wonder about the family." Patient explored his recounting of the incident with the baby cited above. This writer observed that the patient appeared more reflective than anxious in describing the incident, which was different from the index trauma involving a *small child processed during treatment. Patient replied that he was unaware of this difference.*

***Patient reported an increase in anxiety on Sunday, noting, "I was very anxious all day. I woke up that way." Patient stated that possible triggers included his father-in-law being in the hospital. Patient also reported having a partial memory about an incident during deployment involving comforting a soldier who came through the ER. Patient said, "I'm holding his hand, and he says he doesn't want to die. I reassured him." Patient said he was unsure if this particular incident occurred, although noted it was a common occurrence for him. Patient said, "Is this a real memory or what?" and "I don't know why it came to my mind."

***Patient asked this writer about how he manages to work with so many people who have trauma. Patient said, "I worry about you? You seem to be having a hard time this morning." This writer explored the patient's perception of having a hard time and how that impacted the therapeutic process. This writer asked the patient to reflect on how his concern for others often hinders his ability to focus on his own needs.

The patient complained he suffered a relapse of anxiety two months ago. Today feels "anxiety-ridden." He feels anxious all the time, has difficulty finding words when he speaks (distracted by anxiety), and feels the anxiety is becoming progressively worse. The patient complained he is feeling tired, depressed, emotional, and irritable. He has been snapping at people.

He has been having "lots of thoughts and feelings" about previous deployment trauma. He complained of daily intrusive recollections and fears dealing with similar trauma on deployment. He has trouble sleeping, wakes up having disturbing dreams that he doesn't remember, and feels spent, tired during the day.

***Patient is a chaplain with three problems:

(1) The first is a slight tremor of his hands. This has been present for years but seems to have increased over the last 2-3 months. It affects him mostly when he is holding objects trying to keep them steady. It does not interfere with eating, dressing, or ADLs (Activities of Daily Living).

(2) The second problem is an intermittent loss of awareness but not LOC. These are brief. His wife does note that his memory is changing in the last six months. He seems to forget discussions and even rarely appointments.

(3) Finally, he notes problems with word finding. He "makes his living speaking" but now needs to really think about words, when before he was very fluent.

These notes provide a snapshot of what takes place in therapy. I would be in a dire situation if not for sessions like these along the way. I would be lying if I said I could maneuver this battle alone. Therapy with a professional provides the most possibilities for healing and hope. No matter how much we want to move forward, we need proven approaches to progress. Too often we depend on ourselves for healing. It gives us a sense of control, but it's all too often difficult to achieve. Although we feel lonely, it does not mean we are alone. If we accept that premise, then solving some of our problems requires us to seek help from trained professionals.

One such proven approach is solution-focused therapy. Practically everything we experience with PTSD is negative. So much so that we can get focused on all the negative things in our lives and very little of the positive parts. For healing to occur, we must change the focus from the past to the present and future. Positive thinking is the best way for change to happen. It's important for us to move more from the trauma and all it has done to disrupt us to what we can do as PTSD sufferers to move forward. Essentially, change has to happen in our thinking before change happens in our feelings and actions.

Solution-focused therapy hones in on moving in a positive direction. The overriding belief is that we are our own best change agent in moving forward. No one knows us like we know ourselves, so change begins with us. Any positive change at all is a step in the right direction.

The foundation of this therapy is the miracle question: *If I wake up tomorrow and my PTSD is gone, what would that look like?* One very important part of that would be the heavy burden that would be lifted. I'd be able to live my whole life without having to take medications or miss the things they inhibit. I do mean inhibit because, for the most part, the medications take something away from me.

Antianxiety drugs take away my anxiety…to a point. Medications for mood bring balance to my reactions. Medications to help me sleep put me in such a deep slumber that I don't have nightmares. Feeling medications help me have a more positive outlook. But medications that numb anxiety or anger also have a negative effect on my memory. It's hard to have combinations of these drugs in my body at one time.

Healing in the truest sense is to accept the minor victories that come along each day. It's the ability to refocus when something triggers negative thoughts or actions. If we only accept beating PTSD as being what satisfies, we set ourselves up to lose. Many people prescribe to the idea that not accepting anything short of a cure is setting yourself up for failure. None of us are perfect, and we must accept the fact that we all have flaws. When these things happen, we find ourselves in the same boat as every other person in this world. It's not so much all or nothing as it is that some is progress. Dealing with PTSD is precisely the same in that we will have flaws, we will have setbacks, and we will have failures.

> **Healing in the truest sense is to accept the minor victories that come along each day.**

While it's true that everyone else sees our face, none of us will ever see our own face. All we're able to see is the reflection of our face in a mirror or photograph. Those of us with PTSD may not even be aware of a real problem that exists in that we can't see any of what everyone else sees easily. I believe that is why we have our interpretation of what we think, but someone else has a completely different interpretation. Ours comes from what we intended to say or do, and an entirely different interpretation is formed by what they summarize from seeing the reactions on our face. Those reactions give them insight into what we're thinking or even the mood we're in. We can't see ourselves roll our eyes or make a facial expression and probably aren't even aware of it, but everybody else can, and from that, they often form conclusions.

Not admitting you have PTSD may or may not be denial; it can simply be a matter of unawareness. Many believe the idea of not being aware you have PTSD is absurd. How can we possibly have something so egregious that it changes our personality and outlook and not even know? One reason people are skeptical about the diagnosis is that in their minds, it's not logical!

Take, for instance, that having bad breath affects the people around you. Most of the time, we're not aware of the negative impact we are making. It would help if we were able to smell our own breath, but other than in rare exceptions, most of us can't. Logically, it would seem to me we would always smell the same bad breath as everyone around us. The inability for us to smell our breath is theorized as it would overwhelm our noses to constantly pick up the smell of breath below it, and this would keep it from detecting other odors more critical to safety and survival. The important thing is, as strange as it is, people are not able to smell their own breath.

Depression and PTSD

Depression in PTSD is a condition in which a person feels discouraged, sad, hopeless, unmotivated, or disinterested in life in general for more than two weeks and when the feelings interfere with daily activities.

One important difference is in feeling keyed up versus moving slow. Anxiety leads to "keyed up" feelings, while depression leads to slow **Anxiety leads** motion and fatigue. When an individual **to "keyed up"** is depressed, they may have trouble **feelings, while** connecting with the world around them. Their physical movements may be slower **depression leads** than usual, and they might have trouble **to slow motion** concentrating or following conversations **and fatigue.** that happen too fast.

Tiredness is one of the key symptoms of depression. So is anxiety. Anxiety can make an affected individual feel like they're on high alert. They may notice tons of little details around them and feel like their brain is on overdrive. Rather than struggling to pay attention, their mind may race or come up with catastrophic and unlikely scenarios.

Logically, we know it's possible to have depression without having PTSD. On the other hand, PTSD rarely comes without depression. The trauma itself causes us to be depressed. It's a feeling of deep sadness—a lack of joy from things that used to bring happiness.

All of us are depressed at some time or another in our lives. Whether we admit it or not doesn't affect if we have it or not. One man said, "I'm not depressed; I just lie awake at night and think about my problems." Depression and PTSD go together in that the trauma that causes PTSD also causes depression.

People with depression move slowly, and their reactions can seem flattened or dulled. People with anxiety tend to be more keyed up, as they struggle to manage their racing thoughts. Another distinguishing feature is the presence of fear about the future in people with anxiety. Depressed people who do not have anxiety are less likely to be fraught with worry about future events, as they are often resigned to believing that things will continue to be bad.

There is a loss of interest or pleasure, difficulty sleeping, fatigue or restlessness, feeling worthless, and/or guilt. There are problems concentrating that go along with the feelings in PTSD. There are unwanted memories or flashbacks of those memories. We avoid things that remind us of our trauma. We feel isolated. We have negative thoughts and emotions, irritability, and hypervigilance.

Depression is more intense than not being happy—it's a low emotional state. It lasts for longer periods and has a significant negative impact on our lives. It's difficult to tell whether something is part of depression or part of PTSD. They begin to mix in a cycle, much like stirring soup in a pot. Before long, the things that are separated become part of the mix. There's no distinguishing between the two. Individuals with PTSD are three to five times more likely to be depressed than those who don't have PTSD.

There are cumulative powers and the contraindications of affecting each other and affecting the stupor. When I say stupor, I don't mean in the sense of walking around in a daze—it's more the fogginess of life itself.

Left untreated for a long period of time both PTSD and depression will likely lead to chronic complications. The symptoms will worsen, the quality of your life will decrease steadily, you may have a difficult time holding down a job, maintaining social and familial links and chances are high the people you love the most will also suffer from the blowback of what you're going through.

Seeking treatment will help you deal with all these issues and get back to your normal self.

Nadia Khan,
How PTSD and Depression Are
Connected, www.betterhelp.com

PTSD occurs following a trauma that was so awful that in retrospect you don't understand how you survived. What that causes is an extreme feeling of vulnerability that you get past but that doesn't go away.

Paul Goulston

Chapter 16

IDENTITY

E xpectations are a big part of our lives. They shape how satisfied we feel. When events don't meet our expectations, we're disappointed, sad, depressed, or whatever adjective works for a given situation. We don't want to lower our expectations because that would mean falling short of the mark.

When I foresee the rest of my life, I realize that some of my expectations must be lowered. Those expectations have to do with the emotional side of things. I don't have a doom-and-gloom mentality. I know that if I live much longer, I'll have many beautiful experiences that will make me happy either in the moment or overall.

In my personal life, I am so blessed with the circumstances God has put me in and the people who have been with me—certainly, my family and friends. I can't put into words how proud I am of them.

What I miss the most, though, is that the medications don't allow me to fully experience happiness

As men, we tend to relate more to what we are than who we are. Women, on the other hand, can maintain more of a balance. In other words, what men *do* is usually more important than *who we are*. A man generally receives much of his self-worth from his occupation. So, what has been so important to me over the years is that I was a chaplain. Like many men, because of the way we are wired, I identify with my accomplishments in my occupation.

Most men enjoy talking about their professional milestones at work, their career path, the extent to which they are a leader, and though somewhat clandestine, how powerful they are. That presents a dilemma for me because, for the first time, I'm now forced to deal more with my emotions. PTSD doesn't cause me to not so much be in touch with my feelings, but to be aware of feelings.

Focusing on who I am has always been secondary to me. But PTSD forces you out of that comfort zone. When PTSD entered the equation, I was ill-prepared to deal with what made me tick on the inside. I had lived all my life centered on what I had done on the outside. This introduction into defining who I am is a complicating factor. It might seem odd to some since my life has been spent caring for others. Relationships are essential to me. I love people so much. But there is a distinct difference between caring for others and figuring out how to care for yourself. I continually push down my own needs. It doesn't matter how I'm doing, or who I am. What matters is, am I providing care to others? Do they get something out of our relationship?

But that doesn't wire me in such a way that I am balanced in my life. The most important thing is that what happens to people matters. Whether I can help or not matters. That's why this book matters.

I don't like many things about myself now. I am content, but not joyous. Part of dealing with PTSD is accepting who you are, although you are no longer the person you once were. I fought that. I didn't want to admit that I was emotionally and socially different now.

Paul was saying he could be satisfied with whatever circumstance God put in his life. After becoming a Christian, he endured many trials and tribulations. He was thrown into prison, beaten, hungry, cut off from friends and family. The ability to be content is tied to expectations. If I expect to put all of this behind me tomorrow, I will be sorely disappointed. I can never put it behind me completely, but it doesn't have to interfere with my everyday life or deprive me of fantastic events and joyous situations.

This concept can be hard to understand. The Lord knows I didn't understand it when it had to do with other people. One of the positive things that has come out of my PTSD is that I feel more for people. I think I empathize more because I've walked the same road. I'm more empathetic because I'm less judgmental. I think more about what other people are going through, whether or not I know what that is.

We all have the same types of problems, although our situations may be different. I used to believe in absolutes, but today I see grey areas in many situations.

We have all heard, "Hate the sin, love the sinner." Although we all may subscribe to that idea, I don't believe we're being honest. Many times, I may not hate the sinner, but I feel differently about that person, knowing he has sinned.

That's a positive effect of PTSD. But I still have to deal with life every day...and it's not always easy.

The saying goes, "If you always do what you've always done, you'll always get what you've always gotten." Trying to be a better person is a constant struggle. I know I'm not the same outgoing, talkative person I was for most of my life, and that's hard. On the upside, I don't get wound up with trivial things as much anymore. I don't have to be the center of attention nearly as much, and I don't need to offer my opinion on everything.

I've always wanted to please people. If I ever felt there was a problem with someone, I tried to fix it, because I couldn't stand to have someone upset with me. Now, although I may not behave in the same way or process the way I once did, I have better insight into the complexity of other people's lives.

I saw everything in black and white. Either it was wrong, or it wasn't. Either it was just or unjust. Now, I don't need validation and acceptance as much. The medications don't shape who I am, but *how* I am. PTSD survivors should keep in mind that neither the medications nor the disorder define them.

Many things define me as a person: my relationships with God, with my family, with friends and colleagues. My physical and mental health define me, and so does the fulfilment I get from my work.

I resist falling into the trap of believing that PTSD defines who I am. Because I know it doesn't.

I can't explain how this long experience makes me feel. I know people want to understand, and that it hurts them that they can't.

No one asks to have PTSD, and no one wants it, but that doesn't change the fact that I've got it. It's not easy to judge a person apart from their actions, but it helps to know their motives and feelings. It's harder for me to feel it. It's there, but I feel as though that love is blocked, separated from what's real, what's happening. I know that I can get

No one asks to have PTSD, and no one wants it, but that doesn't change the fact that I've got it.

better, but I also know my limitations. Some of the barriers are beyond my control. I use my coping mechanisms and de-stressing techniques, but I still feel twisted inside.

Identity can both exacerbate
posttraumatic stress disorder symptom
severity, and/or promote positive
posttraumatic growth. Trauma
can also be incorporated into one's
identity, serving not only as a turning
point or reference point, but also
defining one's life and purpose.

Steven L. Berman
Dept. of Psychology, University
of Central Florida

RELATIONSHIPS

I am not the biggest victim of my PTSD. Those I love the most suffer the most.

That's because they, too, live with my PTSD every day. On any given day, my wife has no idea how I'm going to present myself. She must maneuver through life according to what's happening with me. She must weigh whether I am going to be anxious, shaky, or quiet at any given moment. Am I going to withdraw? Am I going to lash out? That's a heavy load for anybody to carry.

Although she doesn't question me other than in her mind, my wife must be thinking, *who is this person and what has happened to the person I love?*

The same problems that plague those with PTSD often plague the ones who love someone with PTSD. Those around us suffer from so many directions. Their love for the diagnosed person deepens their pain for us and themselves. I feel so badly about dragging people I love through so much. The person with PTSD is not the only one on edge—the caregivers are, too.

We're all on a unique journey. What's routine to one of us is decidedly difficult to another. There is no set standard to which we need to conform. We all have the same destination in mind. We take different paths to get there. One of the most disheartening aspects of PTSD is there are no perfect answers.

We should consider that people aren't designed to understand the mental intricacies of someone other than themselves. It's not that they don't have a desire to understand us. It's that their understanding is more about feeling sorry for us. That's not a bad thing—feeling sorry for someone means you care on some level. When that same person is someone I care for or have taken care of, my emotions go beyond sadness and move to hurt. It hurts me for something terrible to happen to them. They're not just a number. They're not merely a name. They are a part of us.

We intertwine our lives with relationships. Some are momentary. Others come and go. It's rare to have a best friend for life. The thing I miss most about military life is the camaraderie. Sure, it's a job and there are jobs everywhere in and outside of the military. But the military is a subculture of its own. We speak a language of acronyms that others don't understand. Not only do we know each other at work, we depend on those around us for our very life, and it's bigger than that which differentiates it from the civilian world. We often live on bases and live next door to each other. We shop in the same grocery store or commissary. We go to the same barbers and eat in the same restaurants within the confines of the base.

There is a city within the local city. We even have chapels, that most times, mirror that of churches downtown. Truth be told, we know many of those around us much more intimately than those outside of the military. It truly is a subculture within our culture. The amount of intimacy within a relationship determines how close a relationship we have. My transition out of the military was much easier than most people would have believed. I spent forty years—which is practically all my adult life—serving. I've had several times when I considered someone my current best friend.

Then…enter PTSD.

I no longer have a relationship with a friend I would consider a best friend. Since I retired from the military a few years ago, I have only longtime friends from the past. I envisioned in retirement that I would have a close, intimate friend, one that I interact with daily, doing things together, relaxing, and talking. Someone with whom I can be totally honest. I would say it's a trickle-down effect of not having much to give in relationships.

We've all heard it said that a genuine friend is someone who knows everything about us and still loves us. While that sounds good, it's not true. It often consumes those of us with PTSD. Thoughts, feelings, fears, and frustrations. I'm not sure that I'm capable of fully trusting someone outside of my immediate family now.

I have never been a patient person. It would be hard for me to be close friends with myself. If a relationship took as much work as one with me, I wouldn't be willing to stay close. Some relationships require too much to maintain.

An element of trust influences everything in life. It determines most actions and reactions. Since the effects of PTSD on the brain erodes trust, it goes to reason that it erodes relationships. Case in point: intimate relationships.

The more we have a trusting relationship, the more possibilities there are for closeness. We share thoughts we would never share with others. Often, closeness has to do with the degree to which we allow ourselves to be vulnerable.

A young woman once walked into my office in tears and asked if she could talk. Before I could even respond, she sat, buried her face in her hands, and cried uncontrollably. In the moments that followed, she fought to keep her composure, apologized for her emotional state, and started telling me her story.

Two weeks earlier, her husband had walked out of the house and had not returned, leaving this young bride and mother of a newborn child to fend for themselves. She didn't know where he had gone and had only received a few short email messages from him. The only certainties were that his life was in danger, and he might never come back home.

The picture she painted is very familiar to many chaplains and counselors today.

Her husband wasn't a deadbeat dad. Another woman had not stolen his heart. It wasn't a lack of commitment and responsibility that took him away. It was his deep commitment and sense of responsibility that caused him to leave. He is a member of the United States Armed Forces, deployed to an undisclosed location, to serve his country in uncertain times. These men and women, along with their families, live complicated lives.

Trauma Effects Whole Families

The impact of PTSD on families is incredible and many times devastating. Not only do families have to watch the disorder affect the individual, but they must also balance the effects it has on the family. The adage that no man is an island rings true with the dynamics of these disorders. Families are not merely spectators, sitting in the stands, watching the behaviors manifested through anxiety disorders with no participation. Families are an integral part. They should be expected to contribute to the healing that needs to take place.

We should remember that the family member's actions with PTSD will affect all its members' lives. A person prone to inappropriate behavior can cause anticipatory anxiety for the entire family at home and in social settings, causing the whole to live "on pins and needles." PTSD within the family might keep the entire family away from certain locations or situations. Those who have PTSD can be very frustrating to family members. These factors seem to demonstrate a definite need to involve the family in treating individuals diagnosed with this disorder.

If and how the family interacts in the treatment of anxiety disorders will have profound implications on healing. Family members can unwittingly act as reinforcements or extinguishers of anxiety disorder symptoms. The diagnosed client needs support and understanding from the family. A supportive family can facilitate quicker positive results. The family members need to know how their interactions affect the one with PTSD and how the disorder affects them.

No simple or magic cure will heal all the pains of PTSD. The behaviors associated with any anxiety disorders affect more than just one person's life. Since they are disorders that affect emotions, they will undoubtedly have a high impact on the lives of family members, friends, and anyone else involved in the diagnosed sufferer's life.

We need to respect our loved ones. They are the ones affected by us the most. They deal with disappointment, discouragement, disillusionment, disengagement, and distrust.

So many people, when they know we've been to war, will call us heroes. My heroes are the family members who not only put up with our affliction but are the very ones to support us. It makes no sense to hurt the people we're closest to. You would think we would do more harm to people we are not close to at all.

My heroes are the family members who not only put up with our affliction but are the very ones to support us.

There they are, every day seeing me at my worst, taking the brunt of whatever mood I happen to be in. My moods change a lot.

The changes or mood is the connection between PTSD and being bipolar. Loved ones don't know when we're going to explode. They do not know when we will isolate or withdraw. When we decide to sacrifice, it's an indication that we believe in what we're sacrificing. Our families make significant sacrifices repeatedly, and they do that because they love us.

My wife endures so many things, whether it has to do with the anger, the isolation, or any other of the negative manifestations I put primarily on myself. The more I become self-aware about my anxiety, the shakiness, the tension, and the isolation, and all these things, the more I can see the affects I have on others. More often than not, people I speak with begin to feel anxious, get angry, and want to withdraw from me. It's a face-to-face look. I'm not the only one that ends up with those same things because it is a cycle. It affects the whole family; trauma always affects the family.

It's tough to explain what this disorder does to you internally. One difficulty of living with PTSD is that we keep our emotions bottled up. Often, we keep things in and try not to show how we are feeling. It's hard to admit how we feel because we know the way we're feeling has to do with the disorder. When I'm having a difficult time, not opening up to my wife feels like being locked in. I want to walk through the door, but I'm afraid to open it.

I'm now beginning to distinguish between my attacks and conflict. I try to avoid conflict any way that I can—especially with my wife. There are many times that I won't say anything because I know it will lead to heightened tensions and arguments. That heightening of tensions brings with it an immediate desire for me to separate myself from the conflict. It's that feeling of wanting to take flight—to get my head back together and evade the anxiety.

Other times I will say something that comes out negative, even though I didn't intend for it to sound that way. That leads to my wife saying, "You're ill," which immediately sets me into a defensive posture. My first thought is *I'm not ill.* I want to disavow it right away. There are times I am right, and times when I'm not. No matter which it is, it doesn't mean that the other person should have to put up with this behavior.

Again, trauma affects the whole family. We tend to unleash the most on the people we love the most. It's not going to be unicorns and rainbows. It's important to accept that causation goes back to us. Once you work through the emotions, that doesn't mean that they won't come back again.

I don't know what my number one answer happens to be, but when it comes to questioning me personally, "why" is by far the worst question!

Connection is Difficult

The idea that frequently comes into my mind when someone says "sensitive" is the warm feelings that have to do with a connection. I feel that someone who is sensitive understands us better. I can be sympathetic or have sympathy for someone's situation and the pain they experience. It's only when we can relate in a personal sense that we can have empathy. Empathy moves us most because we understand that we can feel with them rather than have feelings about them. It is most inspiring because someone understands me. And I desperately want to be understood.

When I believe that someone gets it, the connection that exists is that we can form a strong bond. We relate to each other. At that point I am willing to share more because they don't pose a threat: they don't usually criticize. When someone sympathizes, they are in essence saying, "I know what it's like." In the case of PTSD, we feel more powerless. We have a rather difficult time finding ways to talk, especially about what is happening inside us, without scaring the other person away. We're afraid, and fear is a significant factor.

I'm tentative about asking questions that can be perceived as holding someone accountable, questioning their judgment. Keep this in mind: we judge ourselves by our intentions. Others judge us by our actions. You know what's in your heart. You know what you are thinking. Unfortunately, not everyone can tell how you think and feel. Everyone around you knows how you act. Your life reflects your attitude.

Emotional withdrawal is a way of cutting out people. Often, that means the very people who want to help us the most. It is possible to withdraw without physically moving? Since feelings and the emotions they bring are so important to communicate, it stands to reason I can still be physically present while retreating emotionally. It is an unhealthy coping mechanism that provides a quick fix to keep from being hurt or rejected. It's much easier to withdraw emotionally. The person we are engaged with can't see what's happening inside. When they do begin to sense the disengagement, their reaction is on some level of frustration. We don't want to have the other person shut down.

There were instances growing up where I would fight with another boy. It would begin by putting up our fists in a boxer pose while other kids gathered in a circle; the crowd always hopes to see a fight. Then the song and dance would begin. We would alternate by saying, "Go ahead, hit me," back and forth. Usually, at some point one of us would throw a punch, and the fight would really begin. Yet, often, there would be no fight. One of us would get tired of it and start to back away. Especially when we didn't want to fight in the first place. Backing away reserves some dignity and avoids the fight altogether. The times where I really wanted to fight but didn't really want to engage were frustrating. That frustration would be what ultimately eased the tensions or resulted in my striking out at them.

Withdrawing can solve an immediate problem, but in the long term, it damages a relationship.

The amount of instability and walking on eggshells makes it a rough way to live. It is not easy to live through. Children make mistakes and are readily forgiven. They don't know any better. We tend not to have the same amount of tolerance with adults. We feel they should know better.

I'm reminded that the Apostle Paul said, "I don't understand myself at all, for I really want to do what is right, but I can't. I do what I don't want to—what I hate. I know I am rotten through and through so far as my old sinful nature is concerned. No matter which way I turn, I can't make myself do right. I want to but I can't. When I want to do good, I don't; and when I try not to do wrong, I do it anyway" (The Living Bible). Boy, I can raise my hand on that one. I'm in total agreement.

The act of omission, not doing something, is sometimes worse to the people in our lives than the act of commission, doing something and not knowing why. That's the reason it doesn't matter what is asked—if my answer is, "I don't know," not only do I cause disappointment, but it causes me inner turmoil. I really don't know and hate to be in a place where people question this. I don't have an answer. I could just say, "I don't have an answer," instead of "I don't know," but I don't think that would be any better. It doesn't satisfy me anymore. Because I still can't give a satisfactory answer. It's one of the most frustrating things in my day-to-day life. Some people might say, "It can't be that bad." "It's not right to do the things you do to me and then get to claim to be a victim." That's how cruel it is. I cause heartache to someone else that they must endure. I'm what some might call victimized by the fact that I truly don't know what to say.

That's one of the reasons I don't get involved in disagreements in my family. I'm not great at backing people up anymore. It's a matter of triangulation. My greatest desire is to not be sucked in. If I get involved, I lose with one or the other. Because I didn't openly agree with them and too many times, it means that I'm between a rock and a hard place. What happens next is that I am usually sucked into the disagreement. Let me tell you...that's the thing I hate most about all this inner turmoil.

I didn't want to get help because I didn't think there was anything wrong with me, although I could see it in everybody else. I thought, *I know the coping techniques. I know what to do if I feel depressed.* Yet despite that, I wasn't happy. I was thankful that I'd made it back from Iraq alive, and that everything I'd taken for granted all my life was in front of me again. I had no idea what was ahead, but the difference maker was relationships. It is the connections we make that impact our lives more than any other external piece. Relationships matter!

Chapter 18

A DAY IN THE LIFE OF PTSD

One of the best ways I can think of how to communicate what it feels like to live with PTSD is to open up and share my own experience. To that end, here is what a typical day is like for me.

Eyes open.

Scan my surroundings.

Assess how I am feeling.

My body is sore as usual these days.

My mind feels the same as the day before and the day before, then again and again in the same way.

Well before I put my feet to the floor, the anxiety sets in.

I hope and pray the day will come when I open my eyes and I feel different, but that day has not yet come. I'll never stop hoping against hope.

Get dressed.

Go downstairs.

Open a Diet Rite. I drink these all day. I can't stand the taste of water. Or the lack thereof, I suppose.

Cherri is drinking coffee and greets me, "How are you?"

On this particular day, I don't feel much like talking, and to be honest, the question irritates me. "I'm fine," I answer.

"I'm Fine"

These two VERY LOADED words are typically two words I speak many times every day. Of course, the real truth is that "I'm fine" doesn't mean everything's good. It's intended to relieve the person asking and avoid describing how I feel. Probably no two words are used as often as "I'm fine" in people with PTSD.

In truth, for me, it's a lie. "I'm fine" is a copout, a coping mechanism I use to avoid the truth. "Fine" has become known as the "F" word between Cherri and me. We both know it's a lie. We both know the truth—that I am not fine at all. It's a lie that we trick ourselves into believing is the truth.

I use "I'm fine" because I never want people to feel sorry for me. I do not want pity. I also fear that were I to tell them how I was really feeling, they would never fully understand. And do they really care? Asking how others are has become a sort of habit. Oftentimes we are

174

not looking for an honest response—we are simply doing what we think is courteous.

Can you imagine if we rattled off the myriad of feelings we have in response to the simple "how are you" question? Most people would be dumbfounded. They would be completely shocked at the honesty at first and then absolutely overwhelmed by the information and unable to muster a response. I absolutely would never want to put someone in this awkward situation. So, "I'm fine," it is—always.

I wrote this section on a Wednesday, and then on Sunday, I saw a music video for the first time that summed up everything I said. I don't always understand how these things happen, but I do believe it was from God because it validated my explanation of "I'm fine."

The lyrics say it all.

"Truth Be Told"
by Matthew West and Andrew Pruis
Lyrics © 2020 Highly Combustible Music, Two Story House Music, One77Songs

Lie number one you're supposed to have it all together
And when they ask how you're doing
Just smile and tell them, "Never better"

Lie number two everybody's life is perfect except yours
So, keep your messes and your wounds
And your secret's safe with you behind closed doors

Truth be told
The truth is rarely told, now

I say I'm fine, yeah, I'm fine oh I'm fine, hey I'm fine but
I'm not, I'm broken

And when it's out of control I say it's under control,
But it's not and you know it

I don't know why it's so hard to admit it
When being honest is the only way to fix it
There's no failure, no fall
There's no sin you don't already know,
So let the truth be told ...

Ordinarily, when someone asks how we are doing, we don't want to get into what's wrong. If anything's wrong, we're simply being polite. The use of "I'm fine" characterizes "southerners" and how polite we are—patting someone on the back is more about being courteous. Being nice is not always actually being nice. It's often being polite like we were raised to be.

A friend of mine, Shannon Ladnier drew this doodle at a very low point in her depression. Feeling Intense Negative Emotions while hiding them by saying "I'm fine." The deflecting of the truth is commonplace, even in those without PTSD.

How much do people really want to know?

I feel distressed every day on some level. There are too many balls in the air. Anxiety has been more intense over the past month. I always want things to be better than the happiness that I feel. Although I try to make myself feel happy, it is not easy to do when you feel depressed and anxious. When you are on guard, the idea of being on guard is reacting to practically everything we're talking about what I call hyper monitoring. I would also add something that could be called hypersensitivity. We've got so many things that I don't normally pay much attention to when they show up. Whether it's a phone conversation or a new problem I must face.

My psychiatrist is someone who gives me help most of the time. Someone who is trying to help me, who knows how to do it, was not able to today. Or at least immediately afterward, I did not feel the positive therapeutic influence of my session. The simple fact of feeling depression is to be in a state of mind where emotions and events feel like they are pushing down. So, I dig a deeper hole as depressed feelings send me more and more into a spiral of negativity. All this plays on other PTSD symptoms, such as anxiety and fear, and no doubt isolation. The deeper the hole is, the more I want to withdraw into myself.

Sometimes I feel like what could be described as wanting to have an immediate cocoon wrap around me, shutting out the elements, distraction, pain, and confusion of the surrounding events. Much of it is related to the decision-making process. The more decisions I make, the stronger the pressure. No matter how big or small. Regardless of the impact of the outcome.

I am so good at unintentionally hiding my PTSD. After working in my current job for four years, I revealed something about my disorder. I was having a difficult time with my PTSD and the symptoms. Anxiety, along with the ability to focus and concentrate, were getting bad. After three weeks, I talked to my boss and said I was going to back off from work for a few weeks to get my head clear. I'm having a tough time. Her initial reaction was out of concern. "Why?" she asked. Not to question me, but to gain understanding. I explained what was happening with the PTSD. After that first initial statement of my PTSD has kicked up and is impairing me and making things difficult right now, the first words out of her mouth were, "Your what?"

I replied, "My PTSD."

She was flabbergasted. "I had no idea you have PTSD," she said.

I explained it's not usually a topic of conversation that you bring up. You keep it under control, so outwardly it seems like everything is okay, while on the inside, I can be having many difficulties emotionally. We talked for a few minutes, and she asked, "Would you mind sharing some of this in the staff meeting? I don't think anyone has any idea this is even going on."

At the next staff meeting, I explained to everyone, and when I made the statement, "I'm having a hard time right now dealing with my PTSD," everyone in the room was momentarily taken aback. I could see on the faces and even on the lips of some the same reaction. I was not covering it up, but that is what was happening. Subconsciously, you don't think about hiding it most of the time. There are times when it's vital that you make no mention of it. After four years, they had no clue of what was going on. I opened up about what I had been dealing with for the past ten years. I told a couple of stories. That's when the head of the organization said, "You need to write a book about PTSD. Other people need to hear it."

It may have been a negative situation in that I was hiding something that had been revealed. The Band-Aid had been pulled off. That's the day I decided to write this book. Maybe others would find something to identify within my journey and it would be a help to them. No one wants to show other people their warts and scars. With this disorder, it's possible to be so good at hiding it that others are surprised when they learn the truth.

Those of us with PTSD become masters of deception. Instead of just wearing our masks, we become our public persona. Very few people experience or know the real me anymore. Sharing who I have become is a privilege I reserve for only the most important people in my life. I live life by presenting myself the way I think others want me to be. That's the private part of how I live my daily life. At all costs I protect myself by deceiving others.

It's possible to become so good
at hiding PTSD that others are
surprised when they learn
the truth about your disorder.

Steve West

Chapter 19

LIVING WITH PTSD

Often, people with PTSD have persistent frightening thoughts and memories of their ordeal. PTSD was first brought to the public's attention by war veterans, but it can result from any number of traumatic incidents. These incidents include serious accidents, natural disasters, violent attacks such as mugging, rape, or being held captive. Emergency workers such as firefighters, police officers, and medical personnel are also at risk for PTSD through their involvement in the people they help and their traumatic events and death. The events that trigger PTSD may be something that threatened the person's life or the life of a loved one. It could just as well be something they witnessed, such as mass destruction or tragedy.

Imagine living in a growing community that includes a large university with thousands of students. Leaving your church after a wonderful service of praise and worship, you decide to take your family out for a relaxing Sunday dinner at your favorite restaurant. As you pull into the lot, you realize finding a parking place is going to be a challenge. Thank God, you notice someone pulling out and quickly grab their parking space. Perhaps your faithful church attendance earned you points with the Lord.

You pile out of the car and quickly proceed to the front door. Once inside, you scan the restaurant for any available seat. You spot two empty tables; one is to your left, and the other is to your right. The open table on your right is between a family of six and what appears to be two elderly couples. The empty table to your left is in the corner, but the two adjacent tables are crammed with male college students sporting identical fraternity jerseys. On which side of the restaurant would you ask the waitress to seat you and your family? I encourage you to read the following story while you ponder your answer.

An Unexpected Blessing

After being deployed and settling into a routine, you notice that the days are running together. I can't tell you the number of times I thought to myself, *What day is it?* The life of a deployed military member consists of the same ritual: wake up, shower, eat, work, eat, work, eat, workout, and go to bed. It's the same routine, seven days a week for the duration of your tour. There are no weekends, no holidays, and certainly no vacations. An average day consists of at least twelve hours at work and often even more. Complacency becomes the norm, and you often fail to comprehend God's blessings in front of you.

I'm no different than most people. I miss opportunities to minister and ignore the simplest of blessings that would have changed my day had I been more attentive.

An example of those blessings presented itself one day at our dining facility in Iraq. Master Sergeant Holloway and I had almost finished our breakfast and were enjoying the rare treat of a football game on ESPN. Other than one lone soldier, the two tables across the aisle from us were empty. That suited me just fine, because I wanted to watch the game and enjoy a delicious meal. It was one of those rare occasions when the dining facility was relatively quiet. No better way to start a deployed day. Maybe my faithfulness was earning me points with the Lord.

The peaceful morning was abruptly filled with chairs scraping against the hard floor and weapons clanging as they dropped beside the chairs. The sound echoed throughout the room, the quiet, invaded. Oblivious to those of us eating our breakfast in peace, a group of soldiers sat down laughing and carrying on, making themselves comfortable at the tables just across the aisle from us. Some of us preferred to enjoy our breakfast in peace. I must admit the first thoughts entering my mind were not very Christ-like at all. They were more along the lines of why are they sitting here? There are plenty of tables further away from us. Furthermore, the Army has three dining facilities on their side of the complex. *Why were they invading our dining facility in mass?*

Before you criticize me too quickly, ask yourself if you would be thrilled if more than a dozen college-aged males came in and sat next to your family. Did you decide which table you would choose in the restaurant? Would you choose differently now? Annoyed, I decided to try and focus on the TV. Maybe I could block them out completely.

After a few seconds, I noticed that everything was quiet again. I looked across the aisle and witnessed a scene unfolding I hope I never forget. There, just a few feet from me, sat this group of young, tough, war-worn soldiers with their eyes closed and heads bowed. Not one of them looked around, and each soldier held the hand or locked arms with the soldiers on either side of him. The sound of one lone soldier lifting his voice in prayer broke the silence. After him, another soldier said a short prayer and then yet another. In unison, they all offered a hearty "amen" and began to devour their breakfasts.

When they finished praying, I stood up, went over their tables and told them how meaningful that was to me. And I asked them, "Why do you guys lock arms, bow your heads and pray as a whole group?" Immediately, one of the soldiers looked at me with a smile on his face and said, "Every morning we eat breakfast together and we pray for our food and for safety as we go out on our mission." We had been here for over four months and so far, have not lost one person. I wasn't ready for such a profound answer.

As we walked away, I said to Master Sergeant Holloway, "Who knew we would have something like this to start out our day so inspired?"

I'm reminded that Paul told Timothy, "Don't let anyone look down on you because you are young, but set an example for the believers in speech, in life, in love, in faith, and purity." God often chooses to speak to people in a still, small voice, but for me, it sometimes has to be a hard slap upside the head. Sometimes the Lord has to get my attention first before He can give me a blessing. I'm thankful that He's patient and loving with me and understands I'm a long-term project.

We stopped before leaving that morning and thanked those young men for sharing an unexpected blessing with us. My prayer is that God planted a seed in my heart that will help me when I'm tempted to be quick to judge others. Let's take the time to notice the little blessings in life, those usually insignificant moments that can make a difference in our day. Then, in an attitude of thanks, share a blessing with someone else.

At least I had the presence of mind to take out my camera and snap a picture. I had to move so fast that it's not entirely in focus, but I believe it will give you a sense of the setting. Did you decide which table you would choose in the restaurant? Would you choose differently now?

Piling On

Having a disagreement with someone keeps my anxiety at a higher level. I'd add depression to the mix. Sometimes there are several things that are hitting all at once. Fighting for my attention and the reactions in daily life seems to converge. Multiple things make me feel

> **Handling multiple things makes me feel tense, and when I have situaions that add to the present anxiety, it activates other symptoms.**

tense, and when I have situations that adds to the present anxiety it takes me activates other symptoms.

We think making a mountain out of a molehill is taking something that isn't significant and blowing it out of proportion. When I say to make a mountain from a molehill, I'm saying, you start with one thing and then add something else to the pile. Then putting something else on top of what's already accumulating. You didn't jump emotionally from a molehill to a mountain but starting with a molehill and gradually it gets to a point where it's like a mountain.

I think of it as emotionally piling on. It's a reality, piling on the truth. The problem is that there are times when things bombard me from different directions. For instance, you're dealing with a repairer who's finished working on a problem. The repairman claims that it is repaired, only to find out a little later, it's not repaired. This reminds me of the daily ebb and flow of PTSD. People say that it's like a roller coaster ride, which makes sense. I've even been known to say this, but so many times I accept what the repairman says about it being done and that gives me hope, that makes me happy.

Everything has to do with something that's wrong in the first place, then receiving help. Only to find out I'm wrong. My belief that it's alright is shattered only to reveal but the problem still exists. And that's where it's a good way to summarize PTSD. It always circles back around. I'll go a little while, a few days without feeling much on the way to symptoms. Suddenly they'll come back, and I will try to find a solution.

Major difficulties exist when I'm not mentally prepared for what transpires in my everyday life. Being caught off guard—not being in control—plays a significant role in my day-to-day mental health.

PTSD changes the structure of your brain. Remember to be kind to yourself.

Dr. Molly Wimbiscus

Chapter 20

HEALING AND HOPE

The primary purpose of this book is to help people understand how PTSD truly feels. As such, the focus has been to look at symptoms and their effects. Still, the worst thing I can do is highlight the countless struggles and not offer any hope for getting better. This is extremely vital for the person living with PTSD and those affected by interacting with them. Nothing works better than healing, hope, and faith for positive outcomes. Giving in to the belief that you can't do anything about a disorder is a guarantee for failure and a miserable life for you and those who want to support you.

Sometimes healing and hope are all about inspiration. I walked into the trauma center one day when nothing particularly bad was happening. Several medical personnel scurried around the bay, busier than normal. More people doing different things than with non-life-threatening injuries. When it quieted down a bit, I came alongside the bed. The scene was quite gruesome. Here was a very young lady, barely hanging on for her life.

It turned out that she was an Explosive Ordnance Disposal (EOD) technician who had been involved in a blast. I later learned that she was on a mission to check out an improvised explosive device (IED) with her team. They had supposedly rendered it safe for disposal. She was walking over to the container that would hold it. The EOD has the best protective gear of any personnel due to the extremely dangerous nature of the job. The best I could understand, the trigger had been diffused. But when she was carefully walking over to place it into the impact container, there was a second hidden trigger. Suddenly, it exploded in her hands. Somewhere in the area, someone detonated the device using a cell phone. Her injuries were strikingly severe. I said a quick prayer for her and to soothe our trauma personnel. These repeated situations are tough for them to process. Prayer has such a calming effect.

When I finished my prayer, one of the med techs spoke to me and said, "Chaplain West, her husband wants to talk with you."

"Of course," I said. Her injuries were so severe, and I just assumed they had called him. "Where's the phone?" I asked.

The next words caught me totally off guard.

"Chaplain West, you don't understand. Her husband's in the next room. He's in her unit but was not on this mission. So, they flew him in to be here."

This is one of those times where I showed little emotion on the outside, but on the inside, I was panicking. I talked with him and brought him out to the bed. She was unconscious. It was hard just looking down at her. He stood there and put his hand against her shoulder. And again, his composure. Then he looked up at me and said, "She's going to make it, Chaplain. She's such a fighter. She'll get prostheses and be able to outrun any of us."

I had been attempting to find the right things to say that would encourage him. But the truth of the matter is, he encouraged me. Later they moved her to the back corner bay for privacy. I stayed throughout the night. Him on one side of the bed, me on the other. He was the most encouraging twenty-year-old I could imagine. Although he became emotional at times, for the most part, he talked with me about the kind of young woman she is. In his mind, everything he was saying about her would happen. This would not beat her.

Occasionally, she would come somewhat out from under the morphine. Not enough to feel pain, but just enough to let him know she acknowledged he was there. At one point, she even turned her head toward my side of the bed and mouthed, "Thank you, Chaplain." We talked about several things. It was so clear that he believed in her, and I think she knew it. She survived and went on to give motivational speeches and found ways to help others.

Of course, she also developed PTSD and shares her struggles with people today. This is one of those stories where I received closure in a very positive, uplifting way. It reminds me that none of us who suffer from PTSD can maneuver the intricacies of symptoms and feelings without the help of others. Having supporters who love you and care for you is a requirement for healing to begin.

Healing and Cure are Not the Same Thing

Not to be confused with healing, cure is another term used with PTSD. The word "cure" means that, after medical treatment, the condition, disease, or disorder is gone. While some can be cured, PTSD has no definitive cure. The right treatments can reduce or manage symptoms and the emotional distress it caused. The person will always have the condition but can live a relatively normal life. Often, doctors will say something along the lines of this: "You're going to get through this. There can be healing. What I can say is that you'll never completely get over it and not be affected by PTSD in some way."

The healing process depends on several external factors.

First, the most prominent factor: the inward desire to heal. Doing the work that it takes to fight this terrible affliction, past the inward side of self-care. Working toward a goal is the external part of our ability to make the best of situations. The awareness to recognize our actions. The ability to be aware of triggers that may cause us to adversely affect others. And to be aware of what we say and what we do to minimize the negative emotions that lead to estrangement. This— and so much more—is our part in effectively managing the effects of PTSD. It takes patience, caring, understanding, a willingness to forgive, and a promise to help from others, none of which the person with PTSD controls.

As with any healing, no matter what in our lives needs to be healed—whether it's emotional, physical, relational—it takes work, the strength we gain from being able to dial back the negativity. And often, how much of the support that we get from others is so critical.

The hard part is that healing with PTSD is not visible. It's not like healing a physical wound. When we see how much better someone else is getting, that encourages us to further support their treatment plan. Most PTSD-related healing takes place inside, so it's hidden from others. That's why an important piece in healing requires hope.

Most PTSD-related healing takes place inside, so it's hidden from others.

The most important factor regarding that, for me, is faith. I believe that something stronger than me is invested in me and cares about me—assists and soothes for healing to happen. I first place my trust in God. Those who have PTSD, who depend upon their faith, can have a better outcome. Just like with physical healing. Study after study has shown that patients in hospitals who are prayed with, experience faster healing than those who never prayed with anyone. That belief and hope in a higher power, whether it be a benevolent God or something else, gives us a place to turn in our darkness.

Not everyone can be cured, but they can be healed. If you don't control your emotions, then your emotions will control you.

Emotional healing involves an integration of the fragmented parts of our soul to help us not only understand a past experience but to resolve it fully, so that it has no emotional response whatsoever. With emotional healing, the past traumatic experience will no longer control our thoughts, feelings, and emotions.

Feeling that after medications we should change and not ever regress is a common misconception. I can't comprehend how psychotropic drugs don't make it better. Medications for physical problems work ie..pain relievers for headaches, cough syrup works for cough and congestion. Muscle relaxants soothe aching and painful muscles. Emotional healing is complicated because getting better is not based on a physical injury, it's about the brain.

I would love to work through my healing process, but no matter how much of the pain is healed, my scars will always remain. They serve as a reminder of what I've gone through. This disorder is many times described as having invisible wounds. When someone has a debilitating illness, they can learn to hide it, especially if it's something internal like heart disease, diabetes, or cancer. They're all diseases on the inside of our bodies. We can't show anyone our emotional scars. They can't see the treatments, counseling, and struggles people living with PTSD go through every day. But they are just as real as an outward physical wound.

Writing this book has taught me self-awareness, the awareness of others, and the awareness of God. And awareness brings healing, to a point. It doesn't mean I can change everything—but if I realize something bad is happening, I can back off.

I'm aware of what I'm doing now, but I'm also aware of what's happening with other people who are in front of me. Then, I'm more aware of what God is doing through this. There's a ton of healing in that, too, because it helps me see the big picture.

Why is it that I have my shower temp set to the nine o'clock position in the winter, but then in the summer, I have it set to the two o'clock position? I realize that in the winter, you want it to be warm, and in the summer, you want it to be cooler, but our house's temperature stays about the same year-round. We set our thermostat to about 70. I believe it has to do with conditioning. Our body is conditioned in the winter to run the water hotter. It doesn't matter what temperature is outside the shower.

Our Need to Control

People fall into two categories: they are either thermometers or thermostats. A thermometer only measures the temperature; it reacts to its environment. A thermostat determines the temperature; it controls the environment.

Many people blame their environment for all their negative results. We should never be a thermometer. Be a thermostat instead. Take charge of your life. Nothing alive stands still. Either you are moving forward and progressing, or you are falling back and regressing.

Would you rather be a thermometer or a thermostat? Most people would prefer to be considered a thermostat, but PTSD forces people to be more like thermometers.

We can control most of it. Normally, we do have control of our environment, somewhat, to change our thermostat. The problem is, in certain places, it makes almost no difference. Whatever we try to do, there's no thermostat that works outside the house. I can control it a little by being in the shade instead of the direct sun.

After 9/11, millions of people said they would never fly again—myself included. It was all out of the fear of being on a plane and being in a crash, or someone taking control and crashing it intentionally. What happened, though, was that reality set in after a while. We had jobs we needed to travel for, and we had to move, or we had to see family, so we all started booking fights again. Every time I got on a plane, I would think about the fear less and less. Then, as time continued to pass, I found myself taking flights and never thinking about the tragedy of September 11th.

Many of those with PTSD tend to minimize positive possibilities for the future. In living with something as debilitating as PTSD, it's easy to give in to the pain and suffering we endure. That's the reason hope is so important. Recognizing how far we've already come is harder because we don't feel hope. No matter what, there are still things that bless us. The more we can see the good things in our life, the more hope there will be!

The more we can see the good things in our life, the more hope there will be!

Chapter 21

FAITH

S ince PTSD takes away much of the control you have in your life, emotionally, it's an important element to recognize that God is in control. I shared earlier that I've been asked over the years how people without faith in God make it through life's tragedies and traumas. You would think the answer would be simple, since faith gives you something to hope for and a place to seek comfort and guidance. The answer I usually give people is "it's easier for those without faith." That may sound ridiculous since faith can be such a positive influence when people are suffering from PTSD. How I explain it is, without faith it's easier because people can blame God for everything. They don't have to take responsibility for anything. It's God's fault. If He was a loving God, then He wouldn't make people suffer.

When we don't take responsibility for our actions and reactions, the burden may seem lighter. Some people are very good at the blame game; they can deflect their own feelings on someone else. It's simply somebody else's fault. The easiest path is always to pass the blame to someone or something other than myself. The burden is lighter when you give it to somebody else. The problem with that kind of thinking is they don't learn from their own mistakes. Part of that mentality has to do with the "woe is me" factor.

If I can shift the responsibility and blame somewhere else, I can also become the victim. Paranoia continually keeps you in a negative reactive mode. Again, it comes down to not being able to move toward healing. Just as in life, most things are hindered when we unduly refuse to be held accountable.

My faith is what concerns me most in life, but faith is an elephant in the room with PTSD. Most sufferers don't want to deal with how it affects their relationship with God.

Those who are religious by nature will find it governs most everything in our lives. It doesn't matter whether you believe it or not. Having no faith does not remove the fact that God exists. We can't wish Him away, hope Him away, or order Him away. We can only allow Him to work in our lives as He already does. It's interesting when things are difficult, and every day brings a question as to whether we will live and die that day. It is something that exists all the time.

Then we find ourselves in situations in our lives where we think we are in danger or may absolutely be in danger. Someone wants to hurt us and hopes to find us. We move closer to our faith during a crisis. Whether we believe in God or are religious ourselves doesn't matter. One thing we all know we will face is death, and that we want to postpone it as long as possible and not think about it.

The fact exists that when we are in the most difficult times of our lives, or someone we love is in the most difficult times of their life, or when we are in fear of our lives, a relationship with God becomes paramount. Of course, some people do not believe in God. But I find that there are far fewer people who do not believe in God amid the crisis, fear, and trauma. In those times, people who would never pray, pray to someone.

In times of crisis, fear, and trauma, people who never pray tend to pray to *someone*.

Symptoms and emotions are what people see. The emotional turmoil inside, however, involves fear and guilt. These things can elicit reactions of great significance. There's an old joke from years past about parents who tell their children, "I had to walk five miles in the snow—all of it uphill, both ways—to get to school when I was growing up." While that causes me to chuckle, it relates to the negative conditions we fight daily.

We don't talk much about struggles, but there's a litany of emotions, especially as reactions. I struggle with my PTSD. I've had people say, "You shouldn't feel shame and embarrassment. It's not your fault." Then there are others who take a more cynical approach and judge me because I have PTSD. The prevailing thought is you can overcome it if you try hard enough, or that "if you have enough faith, God will take you out of it."

So often, when someone says they don't understand why we do this or that, the answer is because "I don't know." You can bet that it's not the answer they wanted to hear. There it is. So many things about this are beyond my understanding. I end up saying "I don't know" multiple times when asked "why." It works the same with do's and don'ts. Why did you do this? Why didn't you do that?

I've always loved the poem entitled "Footprints in the Sand":

One night I dreamed a dream.
As I was walking along the beach with my Lord.
Across the dark sky flashed scenes from my life.
For each scene, I noticed two sets of footprints in the sand,
One belonging to me and one to my Lord.

After the last scene of my life flashed before me,
I looked back at the footprints in the sand.
I noticed that at many times along the path of my life,
especially at the very lowest and saddest times,
there was only one set of footprints.

This really troubled me, so I asked the Lord about it.
"Lord, you said once I decided to follow you,
You'd walk with me all the way.
But I noticed that during the saddest and most troublesome
times of my life, there was only one set of footprints.
I don't understand why, when I needed You the most,
You would leave me."

He whispered, "My precious child,
I love you and will never leave you
Never, ever, during your trials and testings.
When you saw only one set of footprints,
It was then that I carried you."

It's great to say: I undauntedly and without hesitation believe God carries me in my worst times. He hasn't abandoned me. He's doing everything He can to help me. That help depends on our willingness to allow Him to work.

A Measure of Faith

My life has always focused on faith in God and faith in those around me. Some people say they have little or no faith. I believe these people are deceiving themselves. When we get into a car with another person driving, whether conscious or not, we have faith that that person will get us safely where we're going.

I don't consciously think about it when I get on an airplane. I don't know how to fly the plane. I know we couldn't be without a pilot and a co-pilot. And so I put my faith in whoever's in that cockpit. Maybe I'll never see them. I'm probably not going to talk to them at all. However, I actively believe they are competent, trained, and alert. I don't sit on the plane all through the flight, afraid the pilot might not get us there. Faith is part of our lives, whether we want to admit it or not, whether or not it's religious faith.

Although there are answers out there for some people, I don't have an answer for the impact of trauma and PTSD and why it affects my faith. I firmly believe in God. I believe wholeheartedly in a personal relationship with Him that I know I have. I do not doubt that He loves me and directs things in my life. Every day, there is no situation in which I feel the need for help and would not pray to Him. It's my communication with God. Although that's true, PTSD has changed me. Perhaps not in what I believe, but certainly *how* I believe.

I can attest to not feeling as close to God as I have in the past. I'm not angry with God or have an ill will at all. I give thanks to God every day for all the things with which He blessed my life.

This is the simplest way for me to explain the increased gravity of having a deep and permanent faith in God and as a Christian believer in Jesus Christ. I live my life in a way that would be pleasing to Him, and then, on the other hand, I have something pulling me in a direction where logic has no place. If I know all these things and accept all these things—it comes from belief. My brain doesn't fight it. I accept that I'm grateful for that, and yet, it's like running with someone holding on to your belt. It slows you down…even though you're putting more effort into it.

It's not that I don't have a desire to serve God. I absolutely do. My passion for serving Him has never lessened; it's as strong as it ever has been. My determination to believe is as strong as it ever has been. But at the same time, my desire to do more seems to be hindered. Quite often, my determination is lacking, even missing at times. It's like carrying a weight on my back that requires more effort. And as such, it slows me down. Much of this can be attributed to a lack of joy in my life. It seems that these two could not exist at the same time, but they do.

It's equivalent to my head and my heart being at war. I know what to do and how to do it. It's just that I can't push myself to put the effort forth. What I'm left with is less of a personal relationship with God in the sense of intimacy, anxiety, fear, guilt, and shame having to do with my spirit's life. I don't know how to put it in words, which may seem strange to many. But again, with PTSD, the emotions are hard to explain in a way that others can understand.

My head and my heart are always at war, knowing what to do and how to do it, but unable to push myself to put forth the effort to bring it about.

An added frustration is that I don't know what's happening or why I have this limitation, so there's no way for me to explain it to anyone else so that they understand. There's just no point of reference with the struggles of faith in my life, and it isn't easy to explain. Typically, having faith in something or someone or a deity is a very positive thing. But there's just no point of reference. With faith and the struggles of faith in my life, it's challenging to explain.

I am weary from my sighing.
Every night I make my bed swim,
I flood my couch with my tears.

King David, Psalm 6:6, NASB

EPILOGUE

O ften, what I imagine an experience will be like differs greatly from what it actually is. When I began this book writing process, I thought it would be relatively easy. I didn't realize I would come out feeling changed.

Explaining how PTSD feels has given life to many of my internal demons. It has forced me to work on symptoms I never thought much about previously. My dad used to say, "Until a turtle sticks its head out of the shell, it will never get anywhere." I feel like that turtle. When I started this book, my daily anxiety level was high, and I still had several unresolved issues related to PTSD. Spending countless hours explaining how PTSD feels has put me in some very dark places, intensifying the manifestations of my symptoms. I've always heard that it's always darkest before dawn, and while I'm not sure I totally agree with that statement, I have learned just how dark the darkness can be.

Having to take a closer look at my emotions, assumptions, actions, and reactions regarding PTSD has also reminded me that it's only when I take a step forward that healing can begin. I wrote *The Bronze Scar* to help others, but I find it has helped me so much more. Now that I've finished writing, I find myself astonished by the outcome. Not only do I feel some resolution, but I've realized I'm not alone in experiencing these symptoms, and that's comforting.

Some people might say this book focuses too much on the problems tied to PTSD and doesn't provide enough information about solutions. But the purpose of this book is to help bring about a knowledge of what PTSD feels like in someone's life. I did not intend to offer solutions, of which there are many. The first step to healing with PTSD is to admit you have a problem. Not recognizing or admitting something is wrong means you can't expect to gain any peace. As in most of life, solving an equation or solving a problem requires that I know what problem exists. If I don't understand the problem, then I can't plan the best possible solution.

Some readers might need this book to come to the realization that they may have PTSD and to hopefully seek help. Some readers might identify with many, or all the symptoms discussed. For them, the road to a new beginning will be taking a first step. (I've always loved the movie *What About Bob?* in which the psychiatrist continually attempts to help Bob take small steps—"baby steps," as he calls them. Acknowledging something is wrong—accepting that what's wrong is PTSD—then confronting the PTSD is the only way to take the first small step.) Some readers might be caregivers of those with PTSD and understanding someone they love or someone they care about might bring about some sort of willingness to care.

The key to experiencing success as a reader of this book has nothing to do with whether you agree with or like the way I've written it. If you gain the knowledge to put yourself in someone else's shoes, you've succeeded with this book. I'm not the authority on or the poster child for success with PTSD. What I am is a fellow traveler walking down the same road as so many others. I'm not the expert, but I am someone who cares.

The famous radio commentator Paul Harvey always signed off the air with these words: "And now you know the rest of the story." Whether you are a person with PTSD, someone who thinks you might have undiagnosed PTSD, or someone who loves someone with PTSD, it is my hope that this book has provided you with the rest of the story.

There is no timestamp on trauma.
There isn't a formula that you can
insert yourself into to get from horror
to healed. Be patient. Take up space.
Let your journey be the balm.

Dawn Serra

PTSD RESOURCES

- **The National Center for Post-Traumatic Stress Disorder**
  http://www.ptsd.va.gov/

- **The National Institute of Mental Health (NIMH)**
  https://www.nimh.nih.gov/health/topics/post-traumatic-stress-disorder-ptsd/

- **Mental Health America**
  https://screening.mhanational.org/screening-tools/ptsd/?ref

- **Moving Forward: Overcome Life's Challenges**—Course for overcoming life's challenges. This VA resource is available for everyone, not just the military.
  https://www.veterantraining.va.gov/apps/movingforward/index.html

- **American Psychiatric Association PTSD Resource Directory**
  https://www.psychiatry.org/patients-families/ptsd

- **Wounded Warrior Project Combat Stress, PTSD, and TBI Resources**
  https://www.woundedwarriorproject.org/programs/mental-wellness/combat-stress-recovery

- **Operation We Are Here**—Christian faith-based resources for the military community.
  https://www.operationwearehere.com/ptsdchurches.html

- **Mayo Clinic, Post Traumatic Stress Disorder**
  https://www.mayoclinic.org/diseases-conditions/post-traumatic-stress-disorder/symptoms-causes/syc-20355967

- **Helpguide, Helping Someone with PTSD**
  https://www.helpguide.org/articles/ptsd-trauma/helping-someone-with-ptsd.htm

- **Everyday Health Resources for Patients and Families Affected by PTSD**
  https://www.everydayhealth.com/ptsd/guide/resources/

- **National Institutes of Health (NIH), U.S. National Library of Medicine**
  https://medlineplus.gov/posttraumaticstressdisorder.html

- **All Clear Foundation Crisis Support Resources for First Responders and Their Families**

  https://allclearfoundation.org/resources/resourcetypes/crisis_support/

- **Invisible Wounds: Understanding PTSD**

  https://www.health.mil/News/Articles/2020/06/26/Invisible-wounds-understanding-PTSD?type=Articles#RefFeed

- **For additional help—**

  www.bronzescar.com

He will cover you with his feathers.
He will shelter you with his wings.
His faithful promises are your
armor and protection.

Psalm 91:4, NLT

Made in the USA
Columbia, SC
29 July 2024

39093575R00134